SELF-DISCIPLINE

*Using portfolios to help students develop self-awareness,
manage emotions and build relationships*

Rob Kerr

Pembroke Publishers Limited

18.95

To Brent up in Fergus.
To Craig way out in Minneapolis.
Two good guys.

Canadian Cataloguing in Publication Data

Kerr, Rob
  **Self discipline: using portfolios to help students develop self-awareness,
manage emotions, and build relationships
Includes index.
ISBN 1-55138-104-4**

**1. Self-control in adolescence – Study and teaching (Secondary). 2. Behavior
modification – Study and teaching (Secondary). 3. Portfolios in education.
I. Title.**

LB1060.2.K47 1999   370.15'3   C98-932985-2

Pembroke gratefully acknowledges the support of the Department of
Canadian Heritage.

Editor: Kate Revington
Cover Design: John Zehethofer
Cover Photography: Ajay Photographics
Illustrations: Constantine Zettas
Typesetting: JayTee Graphics

Printed and bound in Canada
9 8 7 6 5 4 3 2 1

Contents

Preface: The Development of Intelligent Self-Control

> When street gangs substitute for families and schoolyard insults end in stabbings, when more than half of marriages end in divorce, when the majority of children murdered in this country are killed by parents and stepparents ... it suggests a demand for remedial emotional education.
>
> — Nancy Gibbs,
>
> *Time* (2 October 1995)

As we are ringing in the new millennium, fully half of us on the planet are under the age of 21. There is now a global community of young people, many still in school. In *Teaching Today* Brent Sheppard points to a generation of young North Americans who are uneasy with the times — futureless, hopeless, fatalistic, frustrated. Studies now show that up to 40 percent of the kids coming to school have a definable learning disability or significant behavioral problem. Journalist Nancy Gibbs, who wrote the *Time* article "The EQ Factor," is right: there is a need for remedial emotional education.

Teachers must relate differently to twenty-first century kids. The time for Industrial Age authoritarianism is past. That's because the world of the young person is much larger today, there is more mobility than ever before, and children have more responsibility and independence at an earlier age. The old do-as-I-tell-you obedience model doesn't work for Information Age kids. In fact, forward-looking psychologist Jane Bluestein cites strong evidence that "children who are too obedient may have difficulty functioning as independent, responsible individuals in today's work world" (*21st Century Discipline*).

Schooling has changed. Today, most learning is in groups. It is child centred, activity-based, and interactive. Students must be able to work in co-operative learning groups, to solve problems together. This capability is also necessary in the modern workplace. A student who enters the workplace with a short fuse and few people skills is unlikely to do well. The demands of the workplace are changing. School is changing. Kids will *need* to change.

Former U.S. surgeon general Dr. Joycelyn Elders insists that as teachers, as parents, we can't really change kids. Our job, she says, is *to encourage and to guide young people into changing their own behavior.* The best classrooms have a new vision for dealing with today's kids: a vision which, instead of obedience, encourages responsibility and co-operation. The psychiatrist Dr. Rudolf Dreikurs has described this ideal as "the development of intelligent self control, rather than blind obedience because of fear."

Encouraging and guiding young people towards self-discipline — the development of intelligent self-control — is well realized through portfolios. Portfolio approaches to academic subjects have become increasingly popular over the past decade. Portfolios allow students to make meaningful commitments to their learning, to set their own goals, to reflect, and to celebrate their growth. University of Washington professor Sheila Valencia sees portfolios as "strengthening the bond between student and teacher and establishes them as partners in learning."

"Living Proof" portfolios put students squarely in charge of their own learning, of their own growth. There are two distinct parts to the program: (i) the exploration and learning of living skills, and (ii) the management of a portfolio.

The 36 living skills sessions call upon students to explore and learn different strategies for (i) developing self-awareness, (ii) managing emotions, and (iii) building relationships. In Unit 3, Developing Self-Awareness, students learn to recognize and label their own emotions, to appreciate the importance of body language and nonverbal communication, to work with the H-B-R model and see how emotions relate to our self-talk; to distinguish an overreaction from an appropriate reaction; and to see how it is possible for the emotional brain to take over the thinking brain.

In Unit 4, Managing Emotions, students learn to relax in the face of stress and to use rational thinking, humor, and the four-step SAT (Sensible Acting and Thinking) plan as alternatives to manage the likes of disappointment, sadness, anger, worry, and guilt.

In Unit 5, Building Relationships, students learn about active listening, perspective taking, skills in divergent thinking, and the Win-Win plan as an alternative to arguing. Students explore the values of courage and patience in building positive relationships.

The second (and ongoing) part of the program is the actual management of "Living Proof" portfolios. Students set meaningful goals and then document their own growth. They practise reflecting and conferencing and celebrate their successes. Related student sheets are found in Unit 6.

The comprehensive program presented in this book broadens each student's intrapersonal intelligence, emotional intelligence, and relationship intelligence. It fosters the development of intelligent self-control — the foundation of self-discipline. Most important, it requires students to make meaningful choices in their own learning.

> You don't get to choose how you are going to die. Or when. You can only decide how you're going to live. Now.
> — Joan Baez

UNIT 1

A Focus on Living Skills

If students are to learn how to regulate their behavior, they must have opportunities to make decisions on how to behave and follow through on decisions … Allowing kids to be problem solvers, to make decisions, promotes feelings of control and autonomy.

— Professors Johnson and Johnson,
   authors of *Reducing School Violence*

A Focus on Living Skills

Program Overview

Self-discipline is acquired through living skills. The 36 sessions and 36 worksheets on living skills featured in this book actively involve students in exploring, discussing, debating, researching, role playing, creating, reflecting, sharing, and evaluating. From these experiences students will study, question, debate, and apply key skills for living: the development of self-awareness, emotional management, and the building of relationships.

Our own lives are not so easily sequenced or categorized. We are continually developing more awareness, working to better manage some of our emotions, and putting effort into our personal relationships — all at the same time. This triad of living skills might be presented more accurately as a Venn diagram:

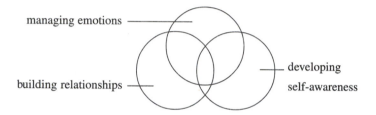

The Interrelationship of Living Skills

In life there is no sequence to learning about ourselves, our emotions, our relationships. These dimensions of our lives are constantly overlapping and are quite interdependent. You, for example, learn an important social skill which may then help you with a difficult emotion which may then lead you to some awareness of yourself. Things sometimes work backwards!

The sequence of the three units on specific living skills is arbitrary. Share this fact with students. Share with students too that there is nothing sequential or categorical about acquiring living skills, about acquiring self-discipline, about growing up. At the same time, the sequencing of the three units and the sessions themselves allow a certain logical flow to the experiences, to the learning. The sessions build on one another; they flow logically into one another. The living skills program, whose core units are 3, 4, and 5, therefore has a logic and a direction.

The first unit of the program, Unit 3, is Developing Self-Awareness. In her *Time* magazine article "The EQ Factor" Nancy Gibbs writes: "If there is a cornerstone to emotional intelligence on which other emotional skills depend it is a sense of self awareness, of being smart about what we feel." So self-awareness launches the program.

Below is a diagram showing the relationship between living skills components of the program.

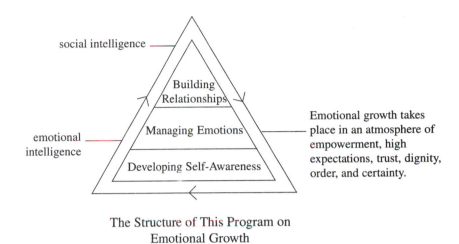

social intelligence

Building Relationships

Managing Emotions

emotional intelligence

Developing Self-Awareness

Emotional growth takes place in an atmosphere of empowerment, high expectations, trust, dignity, order, and certainty.

The Structure of This Program on Emotional Growth

The living skills sessions are concise and teacher-friendly. Each session is built around a skill or concept. There is (i) a lead-in statement, which captures the essence and purpose of the session; (ii) an interesting activity, which helps students integrate and understand the concept; (iii) a worksheet, allowing students to apply the concept and share their ideas in small groups; and (iv) a follow-up reflection for students to complete in their journals. This latter activity serves to personalize the living skill for each student.

The sessions are designed to be about 45 minutes each but can be easily ✓ modified to a little more or a little less. Consider presenting a session once or twice each week. And finally, *do not use the program rigidly*: experiment, modify, go with the flow. As the teacher, you know your students best; you best know the needs of your group; you will see what should be explored in more detail, what should be explored less. Be creative. Be flexible. Most important: *Go beyond the lessons.* Use the concepts and the language in these sessions as a framework for the day-to-day issues relating to emotions, behavior, and relationships. These living skills will be generalized more fully, more meaningfully, as they are applied to the daily lives of students.

Six Messages for Students

The focus throughout the living skills sessions is on learning and growing. Two important themes pervade these sessions: (i) that learning and growing relate strongly to aspects of character (having patience, courage, initiative, reflectiveness, self-respect, and so on); (ii) that learning and growing relate to skills and knowledge [understanding the biology of emotions, learning how to be an active listener, applying the H-B-R model (see page 12) to real-life situations, using the SAT plan (see pages 12–14) to avoid overreacting; understanding and applying the Win-Win plan ...].

Throughout the 36 sessions on developing self-awareness, managing emotions, and building relationships there are six specific messages or prompts made to students: think, own your problems, have a plan, believe in your inherent goodness as a human being, be patient, and have courage.

Think

In *When Smart People Fail*, authors Carole Hyatt and Linda Gottlieb propose: "The question to ask is not whether you are a success or a failure but whether you are a learner or a nonlearner."

In *Emotional Intelligence* Daniel Goleman reminds readers that the human brain has evolved from the bottom up, and that there was an *emotional* brain (the limbic system surrounding the brain stem) long before there was a *rational* one (centred in the prefrontal cortex area). Goleman further explains that thought and feeling are sometimes excellently co-ordinated, sometimes not.

In simplest terms, your emotional brain has the capacity to flood your thinking brain with neurotransmitters, then releasing powerful hormones. These hormones fuel emotions and ignite behavior. Your emotional brain can thus swamp your thinking brain, causing you to act before you think. Goleman explains that this neural high-jacking can occur in an instant — emotions surge before the prefrontal cortex can plug in or mediate the situation. When this happens you are most likely reacting emotionally. You don't think.

Dwayne, a young seasoned criminal, put it this way: "These kids don't think before they do things ... it ain't like they stop to think" (*Time*, September 1994). Most overreactions are impulsive acts of frustration. We would do well, all of us, to learn to better manage our emotional brains, to short-circuit those neurotransmitters, to activate our thinking brains before we lose control!

Students benefit tremendously when they understand the biology behind their emotions. They need to appreciate that an emotional high-jacking, losing control, even for a moment, might bring personal embarrassment, or an opportunity lost forever, or an overreaction they will regret forever. The living skills sessions encourage students to think. In Unit 3, Developing Self-Awareness, sessions 11, 12, and 13, students learn about the emotional brain, the thinking brain, the flooding of the thinking brain and the biology behind their emotions.

It is important that students know that they can interrupt neural high-jackings; they can learn to prevent their emotional brains from swamping their thinking brains; they can learn strategies to better manage their emotions and build successful relationships. What educator Edward de Bono says is true: "It does not matter how good a thinker you may be. It is enough that you consider yourself a thinker."

Own Your Problems

In *The Superlative 21st Century Classroom* (1997) I noted that, unlike traditional expectations, "students in twenty-first century classrooms will not be passive recipients of education, they will be players."

In each living skills session student activities are designed to challenge students, individually or in groups, to apply solutions to simulated problems. Reflecting in their journals presents a further opportunity for students to turn abstract concepts into personal experiences. In their Living Proof portfolios students set their own goals, formulate their own strategies, and reflect and evaluate on their own.

Says parenting authority Barbara Coloroso: "Teaching them to make their own decisions enables them to learn to be responsible individuals who can act in their own best interest, stand up for themselves, and exercise their own rights while respecting the rights … of others." An atmosphere of permissiveness in any home or classroom implies that *no one* owns the problem; an atmosphere of strict authoritarianism implies that the teacher or adult owns it.

The thrust of Living Proof portfolios implies an atmosphere of collaboration, shared decision making, and responsibility. The classroom is clearly a place where students are expected to own their problems, to set personal goals with help, to create workable strategies with encouragement, and to face the logical consequences of their mistakes.

A Caveat About Emotional Reactions

Yes, we will all have problems. We will all encounter sad, unfortunate — and sometimes tragic — events. It is quite appropriate to feel sadness, grief, and sorrow. We don't want to deny these human emotions, nor do we want to suggest that students are "overreacting" if they experience these. That said, we don't want unfortunate events to become chronic or incapacitating.

In Unit 3, Developing Self-Awareness, students are first presented with a simple definition for *overreaction*: you are overreacting if you are becoming needlessly upset, and/or if you act unfairly to others. This is not meant to be a cold, absolute definition. It is, better, a framework for discussion, for thinking about what has happened.

Picture yourself as a twelve-year-old. If your cat dies and you are crying the next day, are you overreacting? Well, probably not. But what if you are still crying a month later? You might well consider this to be an overreaction. Don't blame yourself; that does little good. But you might take a look at what you are telling yourself. What might be adding to the terribleness of it all? You might also examine some workable plans that might help you get on with life in a happier way. Perhaps you could explore getting another pet — maybe that would help.

We should remind our students that life sometimes deals out tragic hands. And it is thoroughly human and natural to feel grief, sadness, worry, and frustration. But we should also remind students that, whatever the tragedy, we all need to move on. We can learn to cope better and move on better if we explore other ways of making sense of tragedies and devise meaningful action plans.

Finally, we should remind students that not all plans work perfectly. In fact, some plans may not work at all! But no one should give up. We should not sit on our problems. Rather, we should share with our students Albert Einstein's maxim: "In the middle of difficulty lies opportunity."

Have a Plan

In *Growing Up Sad* doctors Leon Cytryn and Donald McKnew cite three characteristics of children living with depression: they have low self-esteem, they have a negative view of the past and present, and they see the future as hopeless. In *Humanistic Psychotherapy* the eminent psychologist Albert Ellis makes the point bluntly: "Virtually *all* human disturbance is the result of magical thinking." According to Ellis, if you *think* something is HORRIBLE, AWFUL, TERRIBLE, then it is that, and you will react as if it is. On the other hand, if you take the attitude that the same thing is simply unfortunate — a drag, but not the end of the world — then it becomes just that, and you will react accordingly. Dr. Ellis presents considerable experimental evidence which shows that self-deflating, negative attitudes — *not* unfortunate events in themselves — cause negative emotions.

The H-B-R Model

Students wanting to get better at managing their own emotions and building successful relationships benefit enormously from a plan, a framework for understanding emotions. Developing Self-Awareness, session 9, presents them with a model which demonstrates Ellis's contention that our attitudes, beliefs, and self-talk are more significantly related to our emotions and behavior than what actually happens to us.

In Units 3 and 4, Developing Self-Awareness and Managing Emotions, students are given numerous opportunities to apply the H-B-R model to simulated problems and to their own real-life concerns.

The H-B-R Model

H is the **Happening**: the event which seems to trigger a reaction.

B is your **Belief**: what you believe to be true about what has just happened. Your belief relates to your attitude or self-talk.

R is your **Reaction** to the happening: it has two parts: **f** is how you feel; **d** is what you do.

This model is emphatic that **B** (negative, exaggerated, destructive self-talk) is responsible for overreactions.

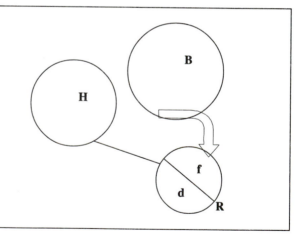

The SAT Plan

The SAT (Sensible Acting and Thinking) plan has been central in my previous publications: *Positively! Learning to Manage Negative Emotions*, the school-wide *Stop and Think: Empowering Students to Manage Behavior*, and *The Superlative 21st Century Classroom*. Students are helped considerably when they learn to identify their own negative, self-defeating attitudes and substitute positive, rational attitudes in the face of unfortunate events. In Managing Emotions, session 6, the four-step SAT plan is offered to students for the first time.

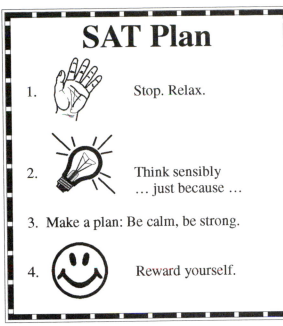

SAT Plan

1. Stop. Relax.

2. Think sensibly
   … just because …

3. Make a plan: Be calm, be strong.

4. Reward yourself.

Step 1: When an unfortunate event happens and you feel strong negative emotions, tell yourself: "Stop. Relax." It may help to move away from the situation.

Step 2: Tell yourself to think sensibly about what has happened. You might begin with "just because (this happened) doesn't mean …" You should avoid negative, unproven self-talk; you might remind yourself to lighten up or make a joke about it.

Step 3: Make a plan to deal with this. Your plan will help you avoid getting needlessly upset and avoid being unfair to others. It will help you to be strong.

Step 4: Reward yourself by saying something positive: *"Way to go … I did it … Good for me … Yes!"*

Students have many opportunities to apply the SAT plan to emotional and relationship problems. The plan offers an alternative to overreacting. When students use it to work through problems they are thinking creatively and assuming ownership of their own problems. They are, as well, incorporating some key strategies introduced in Unit 4, Managing Emotions.

- *Learning to relax:* The first step of the SAT plan prompts students to stop and relax. This step may be the most crucial in preventing an emotional overreaction. Your emotional brain will not flood your thinking brain if you are able to abruptly stop, relax. In Managing Emotions, session 1, students are introduced to a relaxation technique. Relaxing is a skill, and as such will improve with practice. Encourage students to practise this important skill each day.

- *Jumping to the right conclusions:* Step 2 of the SAT plan prompts students to think sensibly about the unfortunate thing that has just happened to them. And in many of the living skills sessions students actively explore ways of thinking sensibly about rotten things that happen to them.

  It is suggested to students first in Managing Emotions, session 2, that many overreactions relate to jumping to the wrong conclusions. For example: If you hear a negative rumor about yourself, you may rehearse some negative self-talk about this; you may convince yourself that everyone finds you unlikeable and is against you. You upset yourself with unproven, negative self-talk, probably jumping to the wrong conclusions about that rumor.

  Students are encouraged to question uncertain information, to be objective, to demand proof of any negative conclusions, and to take a positive attitude about such matters. It is better that they ask themselves: *"What does this really prove?"* When they think sensibly, objectively, positively about uncertain events, they are less likely to jump to dangerous conclusions, to fly off the handle, to overreact.

- *Learning to lighten up:* Students benefit from exploring and practising different ways of thinking sensibly about what has happened to them. A simple cognitive strategy suggested to students in Managing Emotions, session 3, is to *lighten up!* For example: If one student calls another "pin-head," the second student might convince himself that this is "terrible." There's no need for that kind of harmful, exaggerated self-talk, though. Students can learn to tell themselves, *"This is rude, but it's no big deal ... I don't have to be affected by this. Just because someone calls me a pinhead does not* make *me one. This really isn't the end of the world. Good time to lighten up!"* Students are given opportunities to generate different kinds of "lighten up" attitudes. It is important that students actively create their own sensible thinking, that they hear ideas from others. Most often, students themselves are the best sources of ideas.

- *Using a sense of humor:* Authors C.W. Metcalf and Roma Felible are serious about humor. Their claim is that humor allows us to remain fresh and creative, even under pressure; it allows us to work more effectively and to play more enthusiastically. Those of us who have a sense of humor are healthier. Sustained laughter releases endomorphines, the body's own natural morphine. We feel better when we laugh because endomorphines actually ease physical and mental pain. It is impossible to be depressed and to laugh at the same time.

  Humor plugs well into step 2 of the SAT plan. It is a form of sensible thinking, an elated attitude, a positive outlook. In Managing Emotions, session 4, students are given an opportunity to explore humor as a cognitive strategy for managing emotions. Encouraging humor as a healthy strategy is not to suggest that it is a substitute for self-discipline, for hard work, or even for seriousness. However, humor is a way of seeing absurdity in difficult situations, the ability to chuckle at oneself while taking work and play seriously.

  A positive sense of humor endears us to others. It is important that students come to understand that sarcasm is not humor; it is better related to hostility. Nor is teasing true humor; it too has a mean streak. Excessive attention-seeking and showing off is less humor, more denial. Metcalf and Felible cite Dr. William Fry's research at Stanford University: Fry's data show that just 20 seconds of laughter is as good for the heart as three minutes of hard running. In Managing Emotions, session 4, students are given the zany exercise of laughing at nothing. This should get the endorphins flowing!

The Win-Win Plan

In Building Relationships, session 5, students are introduced to a framework for creating positive solutions to relationship problems: the Win-Win plan. They are also given exercises which actively support their ability to apply the Win-Win plan.

The Win-Win Plan
1. Listen actively to the other person.
2. State your thoughts or feelings calmly.
3. Suggest a win-win possibility.

- *Active listening:* As the eminent author and educator Edward de Bono makes clear: "Thinking is not only what you are putting forward but also what other people are putting forward." The first step of the Win-Win plan prompts students to listen actively and reflectively to others. Presenting the strategy of active listening to students is one thing; getting them to practise it is quite another.

Students need to understand active listening for what it is. They need to appreciate its power and importance in their own relationships, and, most important, they need opportunities to practise the skill. In Building Relationships, sessions 1, 2, 3, 4, and 5, students explore, discuss, and apply the Win-Win plan, incorporating active listening, in situations with friends, peers, parents, and teachers.

- *Seeing another's point of view:* In *Teach Your Child How to Think* Edward de Bono shares an important social truth: "People with differing points of view are usually right according to their own perspective." You are not likely to work out a win-win solution if you are unable to take the other person's perspective.

  In Building Relationships, session 2, students first explore perspective taking. The first step of the Win-Win plan, active listening, is inherently about perspective taking. This step prompts students to listen, to understand another person's thoughts and feelings, and to actively communicate this understanding back to the person. Being able to see another person's side of a dispute is a crucial skill in negotiations throughout life; it can be learned and it can be enhanced.

- *Creating possibilities:* Edward de Bono is fast to point out that "thinking is not like our height, not like eye color." He says, rather, "thinking is a skill like skiing, swimming, or riding a bicycle." The skill of thinking, he argues, can be acquired.

  Building Relationships, session 3, focuses on divergent thinking, where students are challenged to create options for dealing with disagreements in relationships. It is not enough to *hope* that students will be creating options for themselves. To believe de Bono, learning to create win-win solutions is improved with prompts and practice. As students apply divergent thinking to simulations and to their real-life relationships, they enhance their own social and emotional intelligences.

Believe in Your Inherent Goodness as a Human Being

Dr. Nathaniel Branden views self-esteem as "the single most powerful force in our existence." However, it makes little sense to *teach* positive self-esteem. Our sense of worth is something that worms its way into us, little by little, over the course of our lives. Or, sadly, it worms its way out. Our self-esteem is likely to ebb and flow. We succeed, we fail; we feel good about ourselves today; we felt rotten about ourselves yesterday. Yet, in the bigger sense, each of us has a private conviction of our own self-worth. We may feel important, significant, worthwhile as human beings or unimportant, insignificant, worthless.

Any young people convinced of their utter worthlessness will face emotional and relationship difficulties. In *Promoting the Social Development of Young Children* Charles Smith writes: "A feeling of personal significance is necessary for children to reach out to the world with confidence." True for toddlers, true for adolescents, true for adults.

We teachers know that we can do much to promote self-acceptance, the conviction of positive self-worth in our students. We recognize certain truths about kids: (i) that they are our social equals; (ii) that they need encouragement, not derision; (iii) that instilling a spirit of co-operation is better than demanding obedience; (iv) that logical consequences are superior to punishments; (v) that it is not the severity of the consequence that matters, but the certainty; (vi) that all of us need to experience success.

We see it in our classrooms: learning takes place when the focus is on the *whole* child. Students need to feel confident. They need to feel safe enough to take risks. Virginia Axline first asserted this almost four decades ago and it is as true today: "The child must first learn self-respect and a sense of dignity that grows out of his increasing self-understanding before he can learn to respect the personalities and rights of others" (*Dibs in Search of Self*).

Be Patient

The simplest definition of an emotional overreaction could be this: *a loss of patience*. When we offer students the SAT plan, we are prompting them to be patient. In the face of trouble, the plan is a bridge between the emotional brain and the thinking brain. On that bridge students practise being calm, thinking sensibly about what has happened, and planning what to do. When students choose to use the SAT plan, they are sharing patience. Indeed, there have been many times when a few seconds of patience would have saved a life.

Patience is key to building relationships. Students benefit when they come to appreciate the power of being patient and when they have opportunities to practise patient behavior. They need to know what patience can look like, what it can sound like. In Building Relationships, session 10, the concept of patience is dealt with. Here, students are given opportunities to apply patient behavior to relationship situations. They are further encouraged to reflect on their own patience in their journals.

Patience relates strongly both to managing emotions and to building relationships. When you learn it, practise it, and get better at it, it helps you to deal with others and with yourself. Being patient helps you change and grow and develop self-discipline. As Harriet G. Lerner writes: "If we want to change, it is important to do so slowly … If we get ambitious and try to change too much too fast, we may not change at all" (*The Dance of Anger*).

Have Courage

The American author Corra May White Harris wrote: "The bravest thing you can do when you are not brave is to profess courage and act accordingly." Sometimes bullied or offended children are counselled to just walk away, ignore the bully, don't say anything. While this is good counsel sometimes, most often it is not. It is not *enough*. Young people need to act with courage and *want* to. So, a better suggestion to make is this: "Say something, stick up for yourself, *then* walk on." Students will gain peace and dignity.

Step 3 of the SAT plan prompts students to make a plan, to be calm and strong. Students must ask themselves: "What can I do to solve my problem in a calm, strong way?" This is the essence of a courageous, peaceful solution — self-control with courage.

In Unit 5, Building Relationships, students are given numerous opportunities to generate courageous plans: in the role-playing activities and in the worksheet exercises. Students develop their own ideas; they get ideas from others. In Building Relationships, session 6, having courage is linked to building positive relationships. The message is this: you can *learn* to be courageous. You can learn to act fairly and courageously with your friends, with other kids, and with adults.

Our students are walking into a tumultous world. One way or another each will make hard decisions about cigarettes, alcohol, drinking and driving, sex, schoolwork, gang membership, pranks, crime, friendship issues, consumer habits, and more. Today's young people won't be helped by moral frameworks which encourage them to be passive or blindly obedient. In a complicated twenty-first century students must be disciplined by the self. They must be able to stand up, stand in, be calm, but be strong. "Face it. Face it," writes American author Evan Hunter, "and it will vanish."

UNIT 2

A Portfolio-Based Program

Our goal is not to change young people's behavior, because that is impossible. Our goal is to encourage and guide each person into changing his or her own behavior.

— Dr. Joycelyn Elders
   Time (December 1996)

A Portfolio-Based Program

Portfolio is a concept, a process: I, as a learner, have a responsibility for collecting my stuff, looking at and talking about my stuff, and deciding what to do better.

— Roger Farr

Portfolios as Tools for Growth

For years developing artists have used portfolios to demonstrate the depth and breadth of their work. An artist's portfolio may include a variety of indicators: samples of work with different media, several pieces which show a specific skill area; examples of growth over time. Sheila Valencia, at the University of Washington, makes the point that these real-work examples are by far the best *proof* of artists' skills, talents, and growth. She says: "With such rich sources of information, it is easier for the critics and the teachers, and most importantly, artists themselves, to understand the development of expertise and to plan the experiences that will encourage additional progress."

Over the past decade portfolios have steadily wormed their way into other areas of the curricula besides art, especially reading, writing, and mathematics. Teachers, too, are using them. About 10 universities and colleges were thought to be using portfolios in 1990; in 1997 the number was put at 1,000. Teacher-writer J. Heidl-Knap writes: "Today's students are used to relying on others, particularly adults, to tell them about their work … Now we must involve students in this process."

Mary Nanavati, head of English at a Canadian secondary school, was asked: How is portfolio assessment different from more traditional methods of measuring students' progress? She replied: "Portfolios bring together what students are actually capable of doing, as opposed to what facts or figures they can memorize." Like most teachers who have abandoned more traditional methods of assessment, Nanavati defends portfolios as providing better "evidence of his or her growth as a learner." Heidl-Knap links a portfolio approach to the development of self-directed, independent learners, who will gain insights into their own learning. "The result," she says, "will be students who show more initiative and interest in their own learning."

Reading teachers, mathematics teachers, and art teachers have identified the key advantage in portfolio assessment: *students have a voice.* Students set their own goals, choose strategies for their own improvement, reflect on their progress, evaluate themselves, and move forward.

Portfolios as Prompts for Reflection

The difference between any scrapbook or file and a portfolio, as educator Judith Fine makes clear, is the *exercise of reflection*. Portfolios and reflections go hand in hand. So we need to help students become good at reflecting.

How do we lead students towards becoming good reflectors? First, we help them identify important questions that relate to their growth as learners. We help them think about the selections they choose which demonstrate growth. We prompt them: "Why did you select the piece? What have you learned about yourself that you didn't know before? How do you think you can improve in this area? What skills do you think you need? What would make this task easier for you?" Then, steadily, we help them generate their own questions.

Teachers Les Nyman and Patricia Wygant caution that building students' reflective skills takes patience but, as reflection becomes more natural, students are better able to judge their own performance. "When we work with students to create these pictures of performance, we take away the mystery, ensure success, and make learning more concrete."

Many educators believe that self-reflection is the most important use of portfolios. The very process of collecting and sifting through documents and materials that reflect student growth gets students thinking about what is working for them, what is not — and *why* they do what they do. Judith Fine says: "Self reflection around their portfolios encourages students to review their activities, strategies, and plans for their futures."

As portfolio teachers our job is to provide time and opportunities for students to gain new information, to reflect, and to conference with us, with each other, and with their parents. The entire learning atmosphere is student-centred. As Heidl-Knap asserts: "We empower children with reflective strategies to help them understand themselves as learners. What could make more sense?"

Living Proof Portfolios

Living Proof portfolios, the portfolios associated with the living skills program outlined in *Self-Discipline*, put students squarely in charge of their own learning, their own emotional and social growth, their own self-discipline. "Living proof" refers to the fact that through their portfolios students will be able to measure, to demonstrate their development of self-discipline. They will set meaningful goals and document their growth. They will practise reflecting and conferencing. And they will celebrate successes in the living skills program, successes measured in terms of real-life experiences — their living proof.

Creating a Living Proof Portfolio

What Will It Look Like?
There is no fast rule on what a portfolio must look like. You may wish to discuss the possibilities with the group.

Some portfolios exist as boxes. Is there a way to organize cardboard boxes to serve as portfolios? Could these be decorated in a way that expresses qualities and interests of the owners? Would space and storage be a problem?

Some portfolios exist as folders, which can also have unique designs. Folders are easily stored and accessible.

Three-ring binders might be best for your class. Binders lend themselves to collecting "stuff" in a neat, orderly way. The sheets and other entries could then be punched and saved in a notebook fashion, probably with dividers to separate the categories or sections.

How Should the Portfolio Be Organized?

Whatever the Living Proof portfolio looks like, it is desirable that it have three distinct sections.

One section should serve as a file for the completed student worksheets from the living skills sessions. Encourage students to take pride in these worksheets, to be neat and to file them in an orderly way. The worksheets will serve as important references throughout the year (and for years to come).

One section should house the reflection journal. Each living skills session requires students to complete a written reflection on some topic or idea related to the session. Lined workbooks, cut in half, work well; these may be housed easily within the portfolio. You may wish to discuss the nature of the journal with the class.

One section should contain "My Living Proof," the vital, definitive part of the entire portfolio — the "stuff" that demonstrates success, the "living proof" of growth.

What Kind of "Stuff" Should Go into the Living Proof Section of the Portfolio?

Students may place anything at all which shows meaningful growth, especially anything that relates to their goals, here. Noting entries on the appropriate "Growth, Reflection, Conference" sheet, found in Unit 6, is important.

What Are the Living Proof Sheets?

The reproducible Living Proof sheets will help students to manage their portfolios. These sheets call upon students to complete a reflection page before each of the three living skills units and to do it again at the end of the unit. There are also three "Growth, Reflection, Conference" sheets applicable to each living skills unit. Students should file the completed sheets in the Living Proof section of their portfolios.

Is It Necessary to Do Every Exercise Suggested in This Program?

No, it is not necessary to do every session in the living skills units. Nor is it imperative to use all of the sheets. Think about the time your group will spend on their living proof portfolios, move through the program selectively, be flexible, create new ideas, have the students create new ideas, and leave out parts which are unimportant now.

The next page, which serves as a handout for students, summarizes what this program is all about. It is advisable to introduce this sheet and review it with students before launching the program.

Your Living Proof Portfolio — What Is It All About?

IT'S ABOUT GROWING! Your Living Proof portfolio documents your growth in three areas: developing self-awareness, managing emotions, and building relationships. You, as a learner, have the responsibility for collecting your "living proof," for looking at it, for talking about it, for deciding what you want to do better. You need to be selective about what goes into your portfolio — it must be manageable as well as meaningful.

IT'S ABOUT LEARNING! As a class we will explore living skills related to awareness, emotions, and relationships. In these sessions we will share thoughts and ideas about ourselves and others; we will learn strategies to manage emotions and to build relationships. There will be large group discussions, small group sharing, and role playing, as well as individual research.

IT'S ABOUT MAKING COMMITMENTS! A key part of your Living Proof portfolio relates to your goal setting. You will be given the opportunity to select goals — a self-awareness goal, a managing emotions goal, a building relationships goal. Though they may change throughout the year, these will be your own important goals, and you should make a sincere commitment to realizing each of them.

IT'S ABOUT REFLECTING! You will be doing a lot of reflecting on what you learn, on your goals, and on your personal growth. A file becomes a Living Proof portfolio only when it includes your reflections. You will keep a weekly reflection journal, you will do pre- and post-reflections for each of the three living skills units; you will write reflections each time you enter some living proof towards a goal.

IT'S ABOUT SHARING, CONFERENCING, CELEBRATING! You will have opportunities to conference with yourself, with other students, with the teacher, and with your parents. Conferences allow you to share your personal goals, to show your living proof, to celebrate your growth!

UNIT 3

Developing Self-Awareness

You cannot teach people anything. You can only
help them discover it themselves.

— Galileo, astronomer and physicist

Developing Self-Awareness

The first part of growth is awareness. It is important that we have a knowledge of who we are and that we acquire a sensitivity about those things that contribute to who we are: our experiences, our thoughts, our feelings, our interests, our abilities.

Awareness, then, is the foundation for change.

SUMMARY OF SELF-AWARENESS SESSIONS		
1	MULTI-FEELINGS	Having fun exploring and labelling the multitude of feelings we all experience
2	MORE MULTI-FEELINGS	More exploring and labelling of our myriad of feelings
3	YOUR EMOTIONAL THERMOMETER	Experiencing each emotion on a continuum from "a little" to "a lot"
4	THE BODY SPEAKS Part 1	Eighty percent of all communications is non-verbal: knowing body language is important!
5	THE BODY SPEAKS Part 2	More awareness activities on how we communicate in non-verbal ways
6	SELF-TALK Part 1	Our emotions are related to our self-talk: what we tell ourselves about what has happened.
7	SELF-TALK Part 2	Our internal dialogue, our self-talk, forms our beliefs, our attitudes about events.
8	BENNY'S OVERREACTION	Learning to distinguish an overreaction from an appropriate reaction
9	UNDERSTANDING BENNY'S OVERREACTION	Overreactions as the result of negative, unproven self-talk or beliefs
10	UNDERSTANDING JANA'S OVERREACTION	What happens to someone may not be as critical as how that person thinks about what has happened.
11	YOUR EMOTIONAL BRAIN	Where do emotions come from? The brain's limbic system is emotional headquarters.
12	YOUR THINKING BRAIN	How are thoughts produced? The prefrontal cortex is thinking headquarters.
13	FLOODING	Our emotional brains can flood our thinking brains.

Developing Self-Awareness 1:
Multi-Feelings

This session, "Multi-Feelings," has students recognizing and labelling a multitude of emotions. Students will benefit from being able to explore, talk about, and label the variety of feelings we all have.

Activity

Play a game of Pantomime-1 in small groups in the classroom, or with the whole class.

1. First, with the entire class, identify and list emotions on chart paper or on the chalkboard.
2. Direct students to take turns with a pantomime, using silent actions and facial expressions, for one of the emotions listed.
3. Ask other students in the class or group to guess the emotion.

Worksheet 1*

Hand out Worksheet 1 and have students complete it. Ask students to share their completed worksheets in small groups.

Follow up this activity by using two or three lengths of chart paper to create a word wall of emotions. Invite students to add to this wall whenever they discover other emotions — from their reading, from television, from their discussions with others. This word wall provides a great reference for emotional development, reading vocabulary and spelling.

Reflection Journal

Instruct students to list as many words about feelings as they can on the top half of their journal pages. On the bottom half of their pages they should reflect on the questions: Do you think developing an awareness of our own feelings is of much importance? How do you think we can become more aware of our feelings?

---

* All 36 sessions outlined in Units 3, 4, and 5 offer student worksheets. These are intended to be completed after session activities. Students can share their responses in small groups.

Multi-Feelings

We have the ability to experience a multitude of feelings. Some of the feelings are *positive*: they are desirable, pleasurable. And some are *negative*: they are usually undesirable, not pleasurable.

PART A: How well do you know your multi-feelings? Put a (+) sign beside the positive ones, put a (-) sign beside the negative ones. You may have to check a dictionary to determine some word meanings.

	confused		ecstatic		exhilarated
	distressed		disconsolate		blue
	elated		exuberant		jubilant
	blithe		dejected		enraged
	miserable		glad		joyous
	cheerful		gloomy		infuriated
	despondent		incensed		frightened
	lively		euphoric		lugubrious
	terrified		horrified		anxious
	stunned		melancholic		depressed
	bitter		affectionate		flabbergasted
	proud		disgusted		ashamed
	let down		content		hurt
	appeased		threatened		ripped off
	downcast		repulsed		flattered
	honored		troubled		sick

PART B: *Word Art* Think of a unique way to write or print the name of one feeling in an artistic way. Here's an example:

Developing Self-Awareness 2:
More Multi-Feelings

"More Multi-Feelings" gives students further opportunities to develop an awareness of their feelings through language. Such an awareness is the foundation for emotional growth.

Activity

Have students play Pantomime-2 in small groups in the classroom, or with the whole class.

1. With the entire class review the list of feelings generated in session 1. Are students able to add any?
2. Let students take turns in Pantomime-2, again using silent actions and facial expressions. In Pantomime-2 the student actually states the feeling being mimed, while the other students in the class or group guess the situation. For example: A student states that she has chosen "frustration." She then pantomimes this emotion. Other students guess the situation. Is she lost in a mall? Is she frantically searching for her wallet?

Reflection Journal

Direct students to peruse a novel they are reading and list in their journals at least 10 "feeling" words. Ask them to add new feeling words to the classroom word wall. Invite reflection on these questions: In your opinion has the author of that novel effectively developed the emotions of the characters? How has the author tried to develop feeling or emotion?

More Multi-Feelings

Here we will explore and use more of our multitude of feelings. Remember emotions are feelings. Some of our feelings are positive, and some are negative. An awareness of our feelings is important in understanding ourselves more completely.

PART A: *Word Search* Read the list of 14 feelings at left below. Then use a highlighter to indicate the ones you have found in the Word Search. The words may be hidden frontwards, backwards, vertically, horizontally, or diagonally. Good luck!

bleak
relaxed
gloomy
forlorn
sensitive
worthless
important
joyful
insignificant
gleeful
dejected
offended
useless
appreciative

p	w	m	h	a	v	r	m	c	t	e	h	b	e	f	u	n	o	o
y	s	q	f	p	x	d	e	j	e	c	t	e	d	v	s	m	o	f
t	e	e	y	p	v	q	m	l	c	o	m	t	u	f	e	n	h	f
b	n	r	o	r	b	m	e	e	a	r	l	o	b	s	l	r	p	e
d	s	q	l	e	g	y	d	p	y	x	m	t	f	s	e	w	p	n
e	i	a	u	c	b	l	f	f	p	d	e	d	e	e	s	n	n	d
f	t	s	f	i	b	l	e	a	k	a	u	d	t	l	s	o	r	e
b	i	a	y	a	v	i	v	e	w	x	y	s	j	h	j	n	o	d
j	v	g	o	t	x	o	h	e	f	z	c	m	g	t	o	o	l	r
l	e	z	j	i	q	r	j	u	n	u	r	a	o	r	i	h	r	t
i	o	z	h	b	x	l	l	h	e	z	l	g	e	o	p	j	o	y
k	b	z	i	e	k	u	k	j	k	r	i	h	b	w	l	k	f	k
j	i	n	s	i	g	n	i	f	i	c	a	n	t	a	g	g	k	j
j	k	r	r	e	t	n	a	t	r	o	p	m	i	m	m	e	q	c

PART B: Use the italicized words in a way that shows you know the *exact* meaning. Refer to the dictionary if necessary!

1. Jerry became *forlorn* when _____

2. He was always *offended* when _____

3. Gina felt *gleeful* when _____

4. Mom became *dejected* when _____

5. She felt *appreciative* when _____

6. Brennan felt *important* when _____

7. Aunt Ida was *sensitive* about _____

8. His *bleak* disposition was the result of _____

Developing Self-Awareness 3:
Your Emotional Thermometer

This session requires students to think about each emotion as existing on a continuum. When they experience emotion, it is not one fixed feeling. Each emotion can be experienced to a greater or lesser extent. As they understand that their emotions have complexity, they become emotionally smarter, more sophisticated, more alert.

Activity

Take a look at the emotional thermometer on worksheet 3. Briefly sketch this on a chalkboard or on chart paper for the following activity.

1. Invite a student to come to the front of the room. She selects one emotion to take her emotional temperature. (Example: "I choose *upset*.")
2. Other students then present a *situation* to her and ask her how much of that emotion she would experience in that situation. (Example: "How upset would you be if someone made fun of your clothes?")
3. She responds with a number on the thermometer: "0" expressing none of that emotion for that situation, "50" expressing a considerable amount, and "100" a great deal. The student may choose any number from 0 to 100 on the emotional thermometer. (Example: "I would be about 75 upset if someone made fun of my clothes.")
4. Have students take turns at the front. You will likely want to limit the questions to two or three per student and set some ethical guidelines for questions.

Reflection Journal

Ask students to check someone at home on the emotional thermometer. Tell them to prepare 10 questions, conduct the quiz at home, and then write their personal reflections on what they found.

Your Emotional Thermometer

When it started to rain on Saturday morning, Niki became a *little* gloomy. Her emotional thermometer registered low (only about 20) for gloominess.

0 ▨▨▨▨▨▨▨▨▨▨▨▨▨▨▨▨▨▨▨▨▨▨ 100

When Toni noticed the Saturday morning rain, he became *extremely* gloomy. His emotional thermometer registered quite high (about 85) for gloominess.

0 ▨▨▨▨▨▨▨▨▨▨▨▨▨▨▨▨▨▨▨▨▨▨ 100

NOW, DO *YOUR* EMOTIONAL THERMOMETER
Read the emotion word at the beginning of each line: each is presented twice. Then read the *situation* described on the line. Color in your emotional thermometer to show how high or low that emotion would become for you in that situation.

Emotion	Situation	Your Emotional Thermometer
		0 100
excited	Get to go to Disneyland	
excited	Get to have a new pet dog	
despondent	Ripped my favorite pair of jeans	
despondent	Failed a major math test	
elated	Found a $1000 bill	
elated	Got invited to a great party	
disgusted	Spit upon by someone	
disgusted	Saw someone litter	
surprised	Found out we're moving	
surprised	Heard my best friend is moving	

Your turn! Choose another emotion and *two* situations. Have someone do his/her thermometers.

_____   [   ]

_____   [   ]

Remember: Our emotions are not simply there or not there. Our emotions are more complicated than that. You can experience each emotion in various degrees. You have your own emotional thermometer which is likely different from your friends'!

Developing Self-Awareness 4:

The Body Speaks, Part 1

This session helps students understand the power of body language. Eight-tenths of what we communicate is nonverbal: our posture, our facial expressions, our walk, our gestures, our eyes, the tone of our voice. If we hope to have an impact on others, it is important to have an awareness of our own body language.

Activity

On a chalkboard or on chart paper display the following table:

EYES	
POSTURE	
TONE OF VOICE	
FACIAL EXPRESSION	
DRESS	
OTHER	

1. Suggest to students that, like it or not, body language communicates a great deal — in class presentations, in job interviews, and even in dating situations. The chart suggests some very important nonverbal communicators; students might recognize others.
2. Using the chart as a reference, discuss briefly the nonverbal communicators in a job interview. For example: What is the importance of eye contact? What is effective eye contact? Is dress important?
3. Have students work in groups of two to four role-playing a job interview. Let each group create the job, the situation, the number of interviews, etc. Each group should take about seven minutes to plan their role play by discussing who will do and ask what in the skit. It is not important to rehearse beyond that.
4. After each role play use the chart as feedback on the effectiveness of the job applicant's nonverbal communication.

Reflection Journal

Provide your students with a quick, interesting home exercise for their journals. Ask them to turn off the sound on a television program for 5 to 10 minutes, then do a written reflection on their observations about actors and their use of body language.

The Body Speaks, Part 1

Your Tips for Gianni

Here is Gianni. He is 17 years old, and he has a new job as a sports director at a summer program. Gianni will work with children six to eight years old, leading them in sports activities. He wants to do a good job with the kids. Body language may be quite important in his job. Write one suggestion for each question.

Will hair style be important in his job with the kids? Any tips?

_____

_____

_____

When is facial expression important for Gianni? What tips would you give him here?

_____

_____

_____

_____

_____

When he is talking to the kids in a group, what tone of voice would be most effective?

_____

_____

When would eye contact be important?

_____

_____

_____

_____

_____

What tips on posture would you make for a sports director?

_____

_____

_____

_____

_____

Any tips for Gianni about his shoes?

_____

_____

Developing Self-Awareness 5:
The Body Speaks, Part 2

This session further develops each student's awareness of body language. If we are sharply aware of how our body language speaks to others, we are more likely to develop the kinds of body language we want in different social situations.

Activity

Display the following body language table.

EYES	
POSTURE	
TONE OF VOICE	
FACIAL EXPRESSION	
DRESS	
OTHER	

Briefly discuss the importance of nonverbal communication in social situations.

1. Ask students to work in pairs or small groups.
2. Let students choose any social situation where someone wants to create an impact. Examples might be these: presentation of a new product idea to a corporate group; a television ad; asking someone for a date (should be a fun one!); a lawyer making a defence in front of a jury.
3. Tell groups to briefly plan skits, discuss the main character's body language, and present their situations.
4. An idea for today's feedback session is to have each student in the class use the chart to rate the main character's body language. Here is a suggested scale: 4 = highly effective; 3 = fairly effective; 2 = not very effective; 1 = not at all effective.

Suggested Follow-up

Have a lip sync day. Interested students could bring in a favorite recording and do lip sync to the sound. Or, do a completely silent act of a performing group — no music, only actions! Then, discuss the body language that made the act effective. Note: It will be important to bring a fun, yet serious focus to this exercise! Students can also reflect on this activity in their journals.

The Body Speaks, Part 2

LUCIE IS NERVOUS!

Yes, Lucie is nervous. She and Johnny have been dating for a month, and tonight she is going to meet Johnny's parents for the first time. It is important to Lucie that she presents herself well, that Johnny's parents respect her. She wants to be confident and sincere. She knows, too, that body language is important!

LUCIE IS OPEN TO SUGGESTIONS: In this space offer some suggestions to Lucie. (a) Make a drawing of Lucie and (b) supply important notes for her, for example, about what she should wear. Make suggestions about anything you think will be important: eye contact, voice, posture. What other aspects of body language should Lucie focus on for this special night?

Developing Self-Awareness 6:
Self-Talk, Part 1

"Self-Talk: Part 1" develops students' awareness of their own internal dialogue, their self-talk. Students will come to realize that we often have very different attitudes, beliefs, and self-talk about the same event!

The feelings we experience are intricately tied to our attitudes, our beliefs: the things we tell ourselves when certain things happen to us.

Activity

1. Explain to students that we are constantly "talking to ourselves." When something happens to us, we almost always tell ourselves something about that event. Our self-talk helps us to form *attitudes* about what happens to us.

2. Have students close their eyes. Ask them to pay close attention to what they are telling themselves as you present them with a mental image. Read:

   You are at home on a Saturday. When you got up the sun was shining brightly, but soon the sky became cloudy, and now it has begun to rain. It starts to rain harder. You hear the raindrops drumming on the roof. You look outside and see the day: grey, cool, wet. How are you feeling about this day right now? What are you telling yourself about the day?

   Ask students to share their feelings and their self-talk. Were the feelings among the class similar? Were the attitudes similar?

3. Next, tell students you want them to listen to Sharika's self-talk about the rainy day. Read Sharika's self-talk: *"Finally it's Saturday. No school. Great! I'm going to get outside all day. Hey, it's getting cloudy … It's starting to rain. Wow! It's really coming down now! I bet the rainbow trout in McDougall's creek will be biting like mad! I'm going to call Dana and Sandy … What a great day!"*

   Discuss Sharika's internal thoughts. How was she likely feeling about the rain? What was her attitude about a rainy Saturday?

Reflection Journal

Tell students to survey their families on this situation: "It's Saturday and it's raining. What three words best describe how you feel about this?" Students should then record the results in their journals and reflect on the attitudes expressed by their family members. Did they learn anything about their families?

Self-Talk, Part 1

Pippy's Self-Talk

Here is Pippy. She has just been told that her family will be touring New York City for part of the summer vacation. Read her self-talk. Pippy's self-talk certainly shows how she feels about touring New York City on her summer vacation!

New York! This is going to be a drag! Now I won't see my friends ...I will miss the rock festival ...It's going to be hot, crowded ... We'll probably be stuck in the car for 10 hours ...I'll be forced to look after my sister ...This is a total waste of my summer vacation!

Your Self-Talk

Now, assume that *you* are going to spend part of *your* next summer vacation touring New York City with your family.

Draw yourself in the space here and show your self-talk.

Your self-talk should show how you feel about touring New York City next summer!

Developing Self-Awareness 7:

Self-Talk, Part 2

"Self-Talk, Part 2" further develops students' awareness of their own internal dialogue, their self-talk. Just like a rainy Saturday will trigger very different self-talk and attitudes, so will other events.

Activity

1. Have students work in pairs or small groups. Each student in a group should think of a certain event (similar to the rainy day exercise in session 6). One student should then describe the event to the other(s). Here is an example: You are walking in the mall and a group of boys and girls point at you and start laughing.
2. Tell students to write down (or simply tell) their own self-talk about experiencing that event.
3. Let students share their self-talk about the event. Direct them to take turns presenting an interesting event to the others. Encourage students to share thoughts after each. Discuss: Were there some examples of very different self-talk about the same event? After listening to another person's self-talk, did students have a good idea of how that person was *feeling*?

Reflection Journal

Typically, adults and young people have different self-talk and attitudes about some things. For example: It may be true that most adults would probably have some positive self-talk about staying home on a Friday night. Yet, most teenagers would probably have negative self-talk about staying home.

Direct students to list four or five events which, in their personal opinions, would likely elicit very different self-talk by adults and young people.

Self-Talk, Part 2

Flossie and Mannie and Their Self-Talk

An Elvis Presley tune has just come on the radio. Look at the self-talk of Flossie and Mannie.

Their self-talk certainly indicates how they feel about Elvis music!

Your Self-Talk

Imagine: An Elvis tune has just come on the radio. In the space at right illustrate yourself, and show your self-talk.

People may have very different self-talk about the same event. Our self-talk is directly related to how we feel about something.

Developing Self-Awareness 8:
Benny's Overreaction

Students learn here to distinguish an overreaction from an appropriate reaction. We overreact when we become needlessly upset, and/or when we are unfair to others.

Activity

1. Here's an opportunity for you to ham it up a little. Explain to the class that something *unfortunate* has just happened to Benny — his bike has been stolen. Now, role-play Benny's overreaction in front of the class. In your skit, show Benny discovering his bike is missing. His self-talk should be extremely negative: *"This is horrible, awful. I can't stand this! My mom will KILL ME! If I find those creeps, I will murder them!"* You might show Benny wailing away, pounding the walls, kicking at a desk. (The students should find Benny's overreaction hilarious.)

2. Next, explain to the class that Benny has overreacted to this event. On chart paper or on the chalkboard list the two rules for an overreaction: we overreact if we become needlessly upset, and/or if we are unfair to others. Discuss these rules in relation to Benny's reaction to the stolen bike.

3. Let the students briefly plan and role-play an overreaction to some unfortunate event. (You may choose to establish some ground rules so students won't get too carried away.) They will have some fun with these skits!

Reflection Journal

Explain first that we have all overreacted to something. You may share an anecdote on one time *you* have overreacted to something.

For their journal entries tell students to reflect on one time they have overreacted. Remind them to include the self-talk they may have had at the time of their overreaction.

Benny's Overreaction

Remember: When something unfortunate happens to Benny, he might react appropriately, or he might *over*react.

There are two rules for an overreaction. We overreact when we become needlessly upset, and/or when we are unfair to others.

Benny Overreacts!

Something unfortunate has just happened: Jonathon has lost Benny's football.

As usual, Benny overreacts. First of all he is becoming too upset about the football. Second, he is being unfair to Jonathon.

This is HORRIBLE! You are a fool, Jonathon! That was my best football. How could you lose it? I'm going to get even with you for this!

Benny Overreacts Again!

It's your turn. Think of some other *unfortunate* event that might happen to Benny. Write that here:

_____

_____

_____

Then, illustrate Benny overreacting to that event. Be sure to show Benny's thoughts, his self-talk.

Developing Self-Awareness 9:

Understanding Benny's Overreaction

The concise model below, at right, is called an H-B-R. In this case, the H-B-R shows why Benny overreacted to the stolen bike. It strongly suggests that "overreactions" are not caused by unfortunate happenings; they are caused by negative, unproven beliefs about what has happened to us.

Activity

1. On chart paper or chalkboard illustrate the H-B-R model.

   H represents the HAPPENING (some unfortunate event that has happened)
   B is your BELIEF (what you are telling yourself about what has happened)
   R is your REACTION (how you feel **f** about what has happened, and **d** what you do)

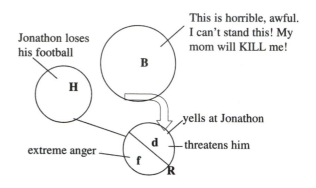

Jonathon loses his football — **H**

This is horrible, awful. I can't stand this! My mom will KILL me! — **B**

yells at Jonathon — threatens him — **d**

extreme anger — **f**

R

   Next, fill in Benny's H-B-R. Strongly make the point that Benny's overreaction was not solely caused by the happening, but instead was the result of his negative, unproven belief or self-talk about having his bike stolen.

2. In the previous session students role-played a character overreacting to an unfortunate happening. Have students do that overreacting character's H-B-R. If students complete these on large pieces of chart paper, they may share them easily with the class.

Be sure to stress that the strong causal factor in overreactions is the character's exaggerated, negative self-talk: unproven, damaging, silly beliefs or attitudes. Overreactions are not caused by events or happenings!

Reflection Journal

Ask students to complete H-B-Rs on the overreactions noted in their last journal entries. Suggestion: Complete an H-B-R on the overreaction you shared with the class.

Understanding Benny's Overreaction

When Benny's bike was stolen he overreacted.

I can't believe this. This is HORRIBLE! It's the most UNFAIR thing in the world! I will KILL them!

Look at the H-B-R model below. It reveals why Benny overreacted.

H represents the HAPPENING (the unfortunate event)

B represents his BELIEF (what he told himself about what happened)

R is his REACTION (how he feels **f** about what has happened, and **d** what he did about it)

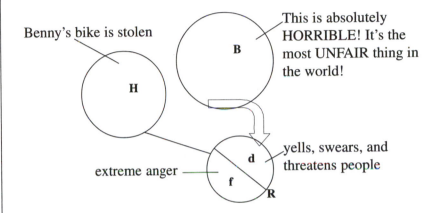

Benny's bike is stolen

This is absolutely HORRIBLE! It's the most UNFAIR thing in the world!

extreme anger

yells, swears, and threatens people

Benny's H-B-R shows something important. Benny's overreaction is *not* caused by the happening! Benny's overreaction is caused by his beliefs — by his negative, unproven, exaggerated self-talk.

Benny went to the barber for a haircut, but became very, *very* UPSET!

Draw Benny and his bad haircut.

Now, in this space draw and write Benny's H-B-R for his bad haircut.

Developing Self-Awareness 10:
Understanding Jana's Reaction

Jana's H-B-R will show how her "sensible" self-talk will result in an appropriate reaction to the stealing of her bike. It is good to have an awareness of our own beliefs, our own self-talk. It is important that we see how our attitudes about certain happenings relate to how we will react to them.

Activity

1. It's time to ham it up again. Act out a skit showing Jana having the identical "happening" as Benny (in the previous lesson). In your skit show Jana discovering that her bicycle has been stolen. She is distressed, but not overly so. It is important that Jana's self-talk is more balanced, less negative than Benny's. Jana should convince herself that having her bike stolen is indeed sad, but "not the end of the world." Jana reacts appropriately; she does not overreact.
2. Next, complete Jana's H-B-R with the class. Stress the fact that her sensible self-talk causes her to act appropriately. She feels sad (but not crushed); she acts responsibly (not wildly, unfairly, irresponsibly).

Stress again that the strong causal factor in an *appropriate* reaction is the character's balanced, sensible self-talk. If you tell yourself that something is HORRIBLE, ROTTEN, UNBELIEVABLY TERRIBLE, then it is. On the other hand, if you remind yourself that it is simply sad and unfortunate, then it will be that. If you convince yourself that it is not the end of the world, then you can learn to manage.

Reflection Journal

Direct the students: First of all, think about a time you reacted appropriately to some unfortunate event. Then, for your reflection, complete an H-B-R for that reaction.

You might want to complete an H-B-R which reflects an appropriate reaction to some unfortunate event.

Understanding Jana's Reaction

When Jana's bike was stolen she reacted appropriately.

Rats! I really liked that bike. The creeps who stole it really tick me off. But that's the way the world is. This is not the end of the world. It could be worse.

Look at Jana's H-B-R. Remember:

H is the HAPPENING (the unfortunate event)

B is her BELIEF (what she told herself about what happened)

R is her REACTION (how she feels **f** about what has happened, and **d** what she did about it)

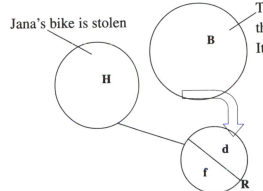

Jana's bike is stolen

This is sad, but not the end of the world. It could be worse.

Jana is not happy about having her bike stolen. But, Jana is able to react appropriately, responsibly to the unfortunate happening. Why? Jana's set of beliefs, her self-talk, is balanced, reasonable, fair. She tells herself that it is a sad day to have a bike stolen, but bad things happen — it's not the end of the world.

Here is another unfortunate happening for Jana. She went to the hair stylist for a cut. Jana thought she had the worst haircut ever! However, she does not overreact. She is unhappy — not depressed.

Draw Jana and her bad haircut.

Now, in this space draw and write Jana's H-B-R for her bad haircut.

Developing Self-Awareness 11:
Your Emotional Brain

In "Your Emotional Brain" students will learn the important biological basics about our emotions. Part of their growing self-awareness of who they are and why they feel the way they feel is understanding their own bodies and the biology behind their feelings.

Activity

1. Discuss with the class: We have done a lot of work so far to understand our feelings, or emotions. In terms of our bodies, where do feelings come from? Is there a physical basis for our emotions? Let students share their ideas/guesses.

2. On chart paper or the chalkboard do a profile of the human head (see page 47). Share with students the following fundamental points about emotions.

> The brain is much like the computer system in most cars, in some appliances, and in our homes. It controls, or regulates, important things. We can think of the brain as having two parts: an emotional brain and a thinking brain. Over thousands of years, as the human brain was evolving, the emotional brain developed first. At the very top of the spinal cord is the brain stem which regulates many "non-thinking" functions, like breathing and metabolism. Ringing the brain stem is the limbic system. Our limbic system operates emotions: love, fear, anger, desire. If you see a tiger coming towards you, your limbic system sends out neurotransmitters (a bit like electrical impulses) to release body hormones (chemicals). These hormones will give your body added energy to run fast. If you see a beautiful sunset, the neurotransmitters may release hormones which calm your body. Neurons and hormones, then, are linked quite closely to emotions: they are related to sadness, happiness, surprise, anger, fear, sexual desires, love, and so on. The emotional brain is related to sensory experiences, neurotransmitters, and hormones.

Reflection Journal

Direct students to do some further research on the biology of emotions. For their journal entries, they should find one or two interesting facts about one of the following: neurons, the limbic system, hormones, an emotion. Also, tell them to write a brief reflection: Do they think it helps us to understand the biology of our emotions?

Your Emotional Brain

YOUR BRAIN, YOUR EMOTIONS:
A BIOLOGY LESSON
Does your brain have anything to do with your emotions? Yes! Here is how it works.

At the top of your spinal cord is your brain stem. Your brain stem regulates many non-thinking functions like your breathing and your body metabolism. There is also a nerve system that forms a ring around the brain stem: the limbic system. All of your emotions are regulated in the limbic system of your brain: feelings of love, hate, anger, desire, surprise, sadness, delight … all of your feelings. If you see a poisonous snake your limbic system wants to alert your body! It sends out neurotransmitters (a bit like electrical impulses) to release body hormones (chemicals). There are various kinds of hormones in your body. Certain hormones calm your body, slow it down. Some hormones bring a sense of love or desire. And some hormones will charge your body with energy to run or to fight. What kind of hormones do you think the poisonous snake will provoke?

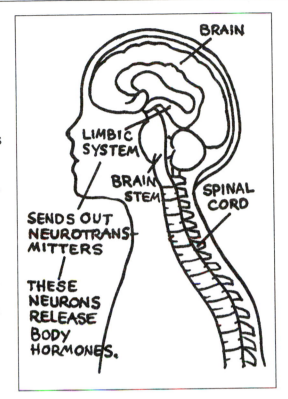

"FREEZING UP": Do some situations cause you to "freeze up," to become so frightened that you cannot even move? It is important to remember that our emotional responses took thousands of years to develop. For eons our emotions have had real purposes. Try to imagine living ten thousand years ago. Why would "freezing up" be an efficient, helpful thing in some cases? In the space below (a) do a drawing of a cave person in danger, and (b) use the key words at the side to explain how the "freezing up" response is triggered.

> Key Words
>
> brain stem
> limbic system
> neurotransmitters
> hormones
> freeze up

Developing Self-Awareness 12:

Your Thinking Brain

In "Your Thinking Brain" students will learn the important biological basics about cognitions. Some animal organisms survive on their emotions: their limbic system triggers hairtrigger responses; they react on instinct; they have no ability for rational thought. As human beings, we are capable of thinking about events, considering options, and controlling our own emotions.

Activity

1. Ask students to share their ideas about this question: Are all living organisms capable of complex thinking (of thinking about what they are doing, seeing options, making choices)?
2. On chart paper or the chalkboard work again with the profile of the human head. Share with students the following fundamental points about our cognitions.

   As the human brain evolved, the top layers making up the neo-cortex developed last. The prefrontal cortex is the part of the brain which regulates higher order thinking. Human beings have a large prefrontal cortex.

   Some animal organisms (e.g., fish, reptiles) have no neo-cortex; they have hairtrigger responses to sights, smells, sounds, vibrations; they react without thinking. Lower-order animals are incapable of child rearing and may eat their young.

3. Instruct students to work in groups; each group should have a piece of chart paper and a marker. Task: To list 10 animal organisms in order of their "thinking ability," from most basic to most highly developed.
4. After 10 minutes have students share their lists.

Reflection Journal

Ask students to list in their journals five thinking operations of which only human beings are capable. Have them reflect: Is it easier living life as one of the world's highly intelligent creatures? Or, do less intelligent animal species have it easier?

Your Thinking Brain

YOUR BRAIN AND YOUR THINKING:
A BIOLOGY LESSON

Thousands of years ago our emotional brain (the limbic system) was well developed, but our thinking brain was not.

But as humans evolved, so did the brain. While the brain stem and the entire *limbic system* developed first, the top layers making up the *neo-cortex* developed last. The *prefrontal cortex* is that part of the brain which regulates higher-order thinking. As a human being, you have a large prefrontal cortex. You have the ability to analyse situations, create options, make complicated decisions.

Lower-order animals (e.g., fish, reptiles) have no neo-cortex. These animals have an emotional brain: they have hairtrigger responses to smells, sounds, vibrations; they react without thinking. They are not capable of love, of affections, or of child rearing.

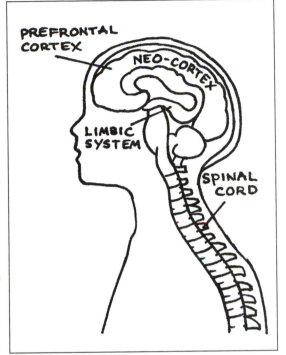

SCENARIO: *Shelly Is Moving* Shelly has just come home from school. Her father tells her that he has had a job offer in another city and they will have to move. Shelly is startled at the news. Her limbic system signals that she cannot manage and it releases hormones. She feels her blood pressure rise, her face flushes, she feels anger. Her body wants to fly into a rage, but she begins to *think* about the situation.

Shelly's emotional brain nearly takes over. But her prefrontal cortex plugs in. Her thinking brain helps her to calm down and to think logically about the move, about what it means, and about how she can manage.

In the space below, draw Shelly and then write in her thoughts, the thinking that helped her to avoid panic, the plans that prevented her emotional brain from taking over.

Developing Self-Awareness 13:

Flooding

"Flooding" happens when the emotional brain takes over the thinking brain. A strong surge of neurons from the limbic system can cause the body to react before the neo-cortex is able to plug in, to "think about" what has happened, what you should do. If the emotional brain "floods" the thinking brain, we may sometimes react in ways we will regret. This awareness is important: Only by understanding the emotional brain's capacity to flood the thinking brain can we learn ways to prevent this.

Activity

1. Explain "flooding." To help students understand the term flooding use the analogy of an electrical short circuit. What happens at home when too many appliances are plugged into one outlet? Talk about how sometimes an event can trigger a sudden and strong surge of neurons from our limbic system. If they are strong and sudden enough, they might cause us to react before the neo-cortex can size up the situation and make a smart choice. The emotional brain can sometimes flood the thinking brain. When flooding occurs, we act before thinking. We are at the mercy of our emotions.

2. Describe to the class one time you experienced flooding. How did you feel afterwards? Are there some times when flooding is completely natural and understandable? Can it be a problem?

Reflection Journal

Tell students to reflect in their journals on one incident of flooding they have seen on television. How did they know the character's emotional brain was totally in control? Remind them that flooding happens when a character is bombarded with emotion and acts before thinking.

Flooding

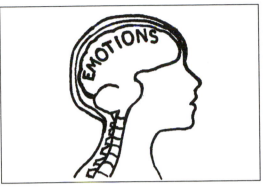

WHAT IS "FLOODING"?

Sometimes an event can trigger a sudden and strong surge of *neurons* from the limbic system (the emotional centre of the brain). If the surge is sudden and strong enough, it may completely flood the neo-cortex (the thinking centre of the brain).

When your brain is flooded with emotion, you will *act* before thinking. You may do something you will regret. You may *overreact*!

Directions: In the space below draw and describe how a Grade 8 student, Tara, might become flooded with a certain emotion. Use the following framework:

The Happening:	Use your imagination. Describe the event that triggered the reaction.
The Emotion:	What emotion did you choose for Tara?
The Biology:	Describe the "flooding" in Tara's brain. How did it happen?
Tara's Reaction:	Draw and describe Tara's reaction. What did she say and do? Did she overreact?

Tara's Reaction: A scene

The Happening:

_____
_____
_____

The Emotion:

_____
_____

The Biology:

_____
_____
_____
_____
_____
_____

Tara's Reaction:

_____
_____

UNIT 4

Managing Emotions

Much evidence testifies that people who are
emotionally adept — who know and manage their
own feelings well — are at an advantage in any
domain of life

— Daniel Goleman,
   author of *Emotional Intelligence*

Managing Emotions

How we feel about certain events is sharply related to our own belief systems: our attitudes, our self-talk. If we tell ourselves that an unfortunate event is rotten, horrible, terrible, then it is, but if we view that event as only annoying or unfortunate, then it becomes just that. We can even help ourselves deal with legitimate tragedies in our lives by developing more positive attitudes, rational self-talk, and by developing action plans.

Students develop self-discipline when they prevent their "emotional brains" from taking over their "thinking brains." Students can develop more control over their emotions by learning to relax, by learning and practising sensible self-talk, and by creating responsible action plans.

SUMMARY OF MANAGING EMOTIONS SESSIONS		
1	LEARNING TO RELAX	Learning to relax as key to helping ourselves manage negative emotions
2	JUMPING TO THE RIGHT CONCLUSIONS	Learning to avoid negative, exaggerated, unproven self-talk
3	LIGHTEN UP!	Learning and practising sensible, positive self-talk
4	LAUGH ABOUT IT!	Using our sense of humor as a way of preventing emotional overreactions
5	BE CALM, BE STRONG	Four words that will always help us deal with trouble: Be calm, be strong!
6	THE SAT PLAN	The SAT plan: A four-step alternative to overreacting
7	DISAPPOINTMENT	Learning to manage disappointing events by using the SAT plan
8	SADNESS	Learning to manage sad events by using the SAT plan
9	FRUSTRATION	Learning to manage frustrating events by using the SAT plan
10	ANGER	Learning to be calm and strong as an alternative to rudeness and violence
11	WORRY	Thinking rationally and creating action plans as alternatives to worrying
12	GUILT	Learning to deal with feelings of regret in a positive, productive way

Managing Emotions 1:
Learning to Relax

Relaxing is a skill students can learn and practise. It is critical to managing emotions and is often the key to self-discipline. The practice session here incorporates imagery, self-talk, and biofeedback techniques.

Activity

1. Lead a brief class discussion: What do you do to relax? Where do you go to relax?
2. Have the class practise the following relaxation technique. Turn out the lights. Read:
Close your eyes. Sit straight in your seat. Head up. Chin up. Focus all your thoughts on your <u>face</u>. With each breath, relax your facial muscles. Relax your <u>eyes</u> so they become heavy. Focus only on your eyes. Now move your thoughts to your <u>cheeks</u>. Relax your cheek muscles until they become heavy. Focus on your <u>mouth</u> area. Let go of all the tension around your mouth. The muscles around your mouth are heavy and relaxed. Now move the relaxation into your <u>neck</u> muscles. Think only of heavy relaxation all around your neck. Feel the relaxation move into both <u>shoulders</u>. Your shoulders have no tension; they are heavy and relaxed. Now focus on your <u>arms</u>. They are very, very heavy, very, very relaxed. Feel your entire <u>chest</u> become relaxed. Focus on your <u>back</u> muscles. Feel all of the tension leave your back. Your back is heavy and relaxed. Your <u>lower abdomen</u> is completely relaxed. The relaxation is moving slowly into your <u>legs</u>. Your <u>upper legs</u> are heavy and relaxed. Let go of all of the tension in your upper legs. Feel all the tension leave your <u>knees</u>. Feel the relaxation in the <u>lower legs</u>. Your legs are heavy and relaxed. Focus the relaxation on your <u>ankles</u>. Your <u>feet</u> are heavy and relaxed. Your legs, your feet are without tension. They are very heavy. Focus only on your <u>toes</u>. Your toes have no tension. They are relaxed. Focus now on your <u>whole body</u>. Your whole body is heavy and relaxed. Focus on your <u>breathing</u>. Breathe slowly. You are relaxed and comfortable. Your head is relaxed. Your shoulders are heavy and relaxed. Your back is relaxed. Your legs are heavy and relaxed. Your breathing is relaxed. Think now of a teddy bear on a soft couch. It is soft and still. Become soft and still as the teddy bear.
3. After the exercise, pause and allow the students to sustain their quiet mood. Then, ask students to rate themselves on how relaxed they were able to become with this technique: 5 = super relaxed; 4 = quite relaxed; 3 = fairly relaxed; 2 = a little relaxed; 1 = not very much at all; 0 = none.

Reflection Journal

Tell students to practise the relaxation technique at home until they become totally relaxed. Remind them to start at the head and move down the body. They should recall the image of the teddy bear to reach a state of super relaxation. Ask them to respond to this question in their journals: on a scale of 10 how relaxed did you get?

Students should become better relaxers as they practise. If at all possible, practise relaxing with the class for a few minutes each day!

Learning to Relax

Learning to relax is not only enjoyable, it's important! Being able to relax allows you some control over your own emotions. And it is a skill. The more you practise relaxation techniques, the better you get. Learning to relax adds to your *emotional intelligence*. It also shows self-discipline!

    Remember: Relaxing is a skill. The *more* you do it, the *better* you do it.

... eyelids are HEAVY ... very relaxed

<u>Directions</u>: In the space below draw yourself practising relaxation, and write responses to the questions inside the boxes.

You in a state of relaxation	What is your favorite place to relax?
	When is a good time to practise relaxing?
	Rate how *easy* it is for you to relax several areas of your body. <u>Rating</u>: 1 = very easy; 2 = so-so; 3 = difficult

RELAXING THE BODY	RATING
The top of the head	
The eyes	
The face	
The neck	
The shoulder muscles	
The back muscles	
The stomach area	
The thighs	
The calves of the legs	
The toes	

Managing Emotions 2:

Jumping to the Right Conclusions

"Jumping to the Right Conclusions" helps students to think sensibly about unfortunate events that happen to them. Most overreactions are the result of unproven, irrational attitudes. We can learn to think more rationally about what has happened to us if we ask: What does this really mean? With some self-discipline, we can avoid jumping to the wrong conclusions.

Activity

1. Read the following story to the class:

   Charlie was walking through the mall. He noticed Shawna sitting on a bench. "Hi, Shawna," he said. Shawna said nothing. She put her head in her hands. Charlie could see her trembling. *"She's laughing!"* Charlie said to himself. *"She's laughing at me!"* Charlie walked a little further through the mall. *"She thinks I'm a jerk! I should teach that rotten Shawna a lesson!"* As he left the mall, Charlie noticed Shawna's bicycle secured to the bike stand. He looked left. He looked right. No one around. He flattened both her tires. That night Charlie's phone rang. It was Shawna. "Oh, hi Charlie," she said. "Listen, I just wanted to apologize for my reaction to you at the mall today. You probably thought I was crazy. I just found out that I failed math this term. That means summer school and all my plans for summer holidays are shot. I just broke down right there in the mall. I'm so embarrassed. Hope you didn't think I was being a jerk."

2. Discuss Charlie's jumping to the wrong conclusions with the class. Suggest that it is easy to jump to the wrong conclusions about things. Ask: How can we avoid making wrong conclusions about events?

Stress that we can avoid jumping to the wrong conclusions simply by reminding ourselves not to. It helps to ask ourselves: What does this *really* mean? What does this *really* prove? We can learn to be patient and ask for proof.

3. Play the game Telephone. The first one in the group reads a phrase on a piece of paper and then whispers the phrase, once only, to the next in line. The second whispers once to the third, and so on down the line. The last person in each line should write what she heard on the chalkboard. Who was closest to the original? This game gives further proof that information is often incomplete or distorted. We should be careful to jump to the *right* conclusions!

Reflection Journal

For their journals, direct students to create a cartoon sequence of a character jumping to the wrong conclusions about something. Then, have them further reflect on this: Why is it easy for that character, and for us all, to jump to the wrong conclusions sometimes?

Jumping to the Right Conclusions

Most overreactions are the result of unproven, negative attitudes. You can learn to think sensibly about what has happened to you. You can avoid jumping to the wrong conclusions about things if you ask: "What does this *really* mean? What does this *really* prove?"

SCENARIO: Zooey is always jumping to the wrong conclusions about things. The other day she was sitting in class. She turned around and happened to see Shari whispering something to Reena. The two girls happened to glance up at Zooey and they began laughing. Zooey said to herself: *"They are talking about me, I know they are! They probably think I'm a real jerk. I hate those girls! I'm going to get even with them for this!"*

Directions: Zooey may very well be jumping to the wrong conclusions about what she has seen. Help her out: (a) In the first frame do an illustration of Zooey, but change her unproven, negative self-talk. What should she say to herself so as not to jump to the wrong conclusions about her friends? (b) In the second frame illustrate what she might later *do* about this.

The girls are whispering and laughing, but what can Zooey tell herself that is positive and careful?	Zooey is curious about what the girls were talking about. What can she *do* about this?

Managing Emotions 3:

Lighten Up!

"Lighten up" thoughts further help students to think sensibly about unfortunate events that happen to them. Too often we "horribilize" unfortunate happenings. If we tell ourselves something is HORRIBLE, ROTTEN, TERRIBLE, then it becomes just that. On the other hand, if we tell ourselves that the same event is simply unfortunate, then it becomes just that. It takes self-discipline, but we can avoid overreacting by telling ourselves to lighten up about some things.

Activity

1. Read the following story to the class:

    Dana found out she was not invited to Carrie's party. *"Oh no,"* Dana said to herself. *"This is absolutely HORRIBLE, ROTTEN, TERRIBLE!"* She stormed out of her room, down the stairs, and ran outside. *"This means nobody likes me. This means I am worthless. I am going to get even with Carrie for this!"*

2. Discuss with the class Dana's overreaction. On the chalkboard do Dana's H-B-R.

was not invited to Carrie's party

H

B

This is HORRIBLE, ROTTEN, TERRIBLE ... nobody likes me ... I'm worthless

gets even with Carrie

extremely angry

d

f

R

Stress that Dana's overreaction was caused by her unproven, negative self-talk: her belief about what it means not to be invited to a party.

3. Have students work in pairs. Task: To help Dana with some specific "lighten up" thoughts. What specific things could Dana tell herself to lighten up?
4. Ask students to share these thoughts. Then, on the chalkboard, complete a new H-B-R for Dana.

Reflection Journal

Instruct students to take a journal page and draw a cartoon of Dana in another unfortunate happening. But, instead of overreacting, Dana decides to lighten up and react appropriately. Tell students to be sure to show her "lighten up" thoughts! For reflection: Do students think Dana can become better at avoiding most overreactions?

Lighten Up!

Too often we "horribilize" unfortunate events. If we tell ourselves that something is *HORRIBLE, ROTTEN, TERRIBLE,* then it is just that! On the other hand, if we tell ourselves the same event is simply *unfortunate*, then it becomes just that. With self-discipline, we can avoid overreacting by telling ourselves to lighten up about some things. Now that's showing emotional intelligence.

SCENARIO: Zak Jacobs lives with his mom; he sees his father on weekends. Last Friday Zak's father promised to take him to the movies, but the father became stuck in traffic. At home Zak began to "horribilize" about this.

Directions: Look at Zak in the first frame. Zak is upsetting himself with negative self-talk. He is actually making his problem *bigger*, not smaller. Help him out. In the frame below draw Zak and give him some sensible thinking. He needs lots of "lighten up" thoughts to help calm him down.

Zak is "horribilizing." 	Zak is obviously unhappy about his dad not showing up on time, but if he can lighten up about this, his problem is made smaller.

Managing Emotions 4:

Laugh About It!

"Laugh About It!" offers one more cognitive strategy for avoiding overreactions. If we are able to sometimes see a little humor in situations, and to even laugh at ourselves, then we will never overreact. In fact, this may take some practice and self-discipline. If we actively remind ourselves to "make a joke" about some unfortunate happening, we have immediately lessened the stress, defused the potential conflict, and displayed a positive social skill.

Activity

1. Read to the class:

   Biff and Joey were on the Hornets floor hockey team. Biff was in goal. The score was tied 9–9 with only 16 seconds left. Joey stickhandled down the floor and missed an open net. A player on the Rockets came back, and with only four seconds left, let go a blinding shot and scored on Biff. Game over. After the game one of the Rockets snickered and yelled: "Hey, we beat you meatheads!" Joey threw his stick, kicked the gym door, and stormed out. Biff simply smiled at the guy: "Yeah, I missed an easy one. I think I must have a hole in my leg!"

2. Using the chalkboard complete the H-B-R for both Biff and Joey. Same happening, two very different reactions. Why? What self-talk/belief do you think Joey was having? What was Biff's?

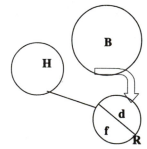

> Stress that Biff chose to look at the game in a *funny* way. He made a joke about his bad play. His self-talk was humorous; his reaction was to make a joke about it. Joey, on the other hand, must have told himself how horrible this was, that he must be worthless since he lost.

3. Next, have some fun with this exercise: to get everyone laughing *at nothing*. Your coaching might go like this:

   Ok, everybody sit up. Now let's see a serious look on everybody's face. Slowly, slowly turn that serious look into a smile. A big smile. Let's see your teeth. Now let's hear a snicker. Everybody snicker. Big snickers. Bigger snickers. Now let's laugh. Bigger laughs. Laugh harder.

   At this point you should join in. Laugh and laugh and laugh.

Reflection Journal

Instruct the students as follows: at home, in your own space, practise your laughing at least one time. Reflect on the exercise for your journal entry. What do you think of this unusual exercise? Is there any value in doing this?

Laugh About It!

If you are able to see a little humor in an unpleasant situation, then it becomes impossible to overreact. This may take some practice! If you actively remind yourself to "make a joke" about some unfortunate happening, you have immediately lessened the stress, defused an argument, and demonstrated emotional intelligence.

SCENARIO: Chrissie's team lost their field hockey game 14 to 2. After the game some of the kids on the opposing team started to razz Chrissie. She said to herself: *"We sucked! And those jerks have got no right razzing me like that! It makes me look like a complete fool! I'm going to tell those guys a thing or two. I hate them!"*

<u>Directions</u>: The top frames below show Chrissie's negative self-talk and her overreaction to the teasing. Your pictures and words in the bottom two frames should show her thinking humorous thoughts about the game and making a joke about this to the other girls.

Chrissie's negative, exaggerated self-talk	Chrissie overreacts. The problem gets bigger!

In her own mind Chrissie sees humor in the game.	Her reaction: Chrissie makes a joke about it!

Managing Emotions 5:

Be Calm, Be Strong!

Be calm, be strong is an important lesson for all students! When faced with an unfortunate event, we can almost always remind ourselves to "be calm, be strong." We can learn to stick up for ourselves, to be assertive, yet calm. If we practise calm, strong self-talk and calm, strong reactions, we will avoid overreacting.

Activity

1. Read to the class:

   Michelle was walking down the hall just before class. She noticed Tom coming towards her. Tom always had something unpleasant to say. Sure enough, when Tom approached he made a comment about Michelle's new outfit. "Hey Michelle, where'd you get that space suit? Are you planning a visit to Mars?" Michelle reminded herself: "*Be calm, be strong.*" She said to Tom: "I like the outfit, Tom. If you don't, tough!" She then walked on, paying no more attention to him.

Stress that Michelle avoided overreacting. Yet she did not simply ignore Tom. She stuck up for herself by, first of all, reminding herself, "*Be calm, be strong.*" She then *reacted* in a way that was calm and strong: she said something to Tom and walked on. She was not overly sarcastic. She did not yell. She did not call him names. She did not become overly emotional. She remained in control.

2. Have the students work in groups to role-play characters showing calm, strong reactions to unfortunate events. Each group should (i) determine an unfortunate happening, (ii) decide on their roles in the skit, (iii) and briefly plan the calm, strong reaction. Tell the students that the characters in the skits should think out loud so we see how their self-talk helped them to act successfully and responsibly.

Reflection Journal

Invite students to reflect honestly on their own abilities to react in a calm and strong way to unfortunate events. Ask: Are you able to be calm and strong about some events and not others? Would you like to become better at this?

Be Calm, Be Strong!

People may sometimes treat you with rudeness or unfairness, and your emotional brain may want to flood you with rage or extreme embarrassment. But your thinking brain can help. You can learn to stick up for yourself, to be assertive, yet calm. Being able to respond calmly and strongly to unfortunate happenings is a demonstration of emotional intelligence. It is also a demonstration of self-discipline.

SCENARIO: Sean and Charlie were walking to school. On the way they passed two classmates who were sitting on a fence by the sidewalk. One of the boys on the fence cried, "Hi pinbrains!"

Directions: Read Sean's overreaction in the top two frames. Use the bottom two frames to show Charlie responding calmly and strongly to the boys on the fence. (a) What would he tell himself? (b) What could he *do* or *say*? Remember: Charlie wants to stick up for himself, he chooses to say something, but he avoids physical and verbal violence.

Sean's self-talk fills him with rage!	His emotional brain takes over. He loses it!
This is HORRIBLE. They're making fun of me. I'm a worthless fool! They are winning. I am losing. I can't stand it!	Sean picks up a rock and throws it. TAKE THAT! He hits one boy on the head.
Charlie reminds himself to be calm, be strong.	Charlie is calm and strong. He stays in control.

Managing Emotions 6:

The SAT Plan

The SAT plan is a four-step, portable plan which helps us avoid overreacting to unfortunate events. Once students have learned the plan, they have empowered themselves. Their emotional brains are less likely to dominate their thinking brains. They have a choice: to overreact or to adopt the SAT plan. The SAT plan allows us to respond calmly, strongly, responsibly. Using the SAT plan is an exercise in self-discipline!

Activity

1. Present to the students the four-step SAT plan. Review each of the four steps. (The SAT plan should be permanently displayed in the classroom.)

SAT Plan

1. Stop. Relax.

2. Think sensibly
... just because ...

3. Make a plan: Be calm, be strong.

4. Reward yourself.

Step 1: When an unfortunate event happens and you feel strong negative emotions, tell yourself: "Stop. Relax." It may also help to move away from a troubling situation.

Step 2: Tell yourself to think sensibly about what has happened. You might begin this with "just because (this happened) doesn't mean ..." You should avoid jumping to wrong conclusions and should avoid negative, unproven self-talk. You might remind yourself to lighten up or make a joke about it.

Step 3: Make a plan to deal with this. Your plan will help you avoid getting needlessly upset and avoid being unfair to others. It will help you be calm, be strong.

Step 4: Reward yourself by saying something positive: *"Way to go ... I did it ... Good for me ... Yes!"*

Stress that the SAT plan is our alternative to overreacting. When we use it our "emotional brains" will not dominate our "thinking brains."

Reflection Journal

Tell students to memorize the SAT plan. They should test themselves by trying to write it down in their journals without looking. Have them check their work. Call for written reflections on these questions: If you were ever to use the SAT plan to help yourself deal with an unfortunate event, what event would that be? Do you think you will try to do a SAT plan for anything?

The SAT Plan

The Sensible Acting and Thinking (SAT) plan is an alternative to overreacting. It helps you to relax, to think sensibly about what has happened to you, to respond calmly and strongly, and to congratulate yourself for staying in control.

Step 1: When an unfortunate event happens and you feel strong negative emotions, tell yourself: "Stop. Relax."

Step 2: Tell yourself to think sensibly about what has happened. You might begin with "just because (this happened) doesn't mean …" You should avoid negative, unproven self-talk; you might remind yourself to lighten up or make a joke about it.

Step 3: Make a plan to deal with this. Your plan will help you avoid getting needlessly upset and avoid being unfair to others. It will help you be calm, be strong.

Step 4: Reward yourself by saying something positive: *"Way to go … I did it … Good for me … Yes!"*

SCENARIO: Carrie went into her room. She found her diary opened. She knew her younger sister had been reading her diary. She could feel herself becoming very angry. Then she remembered the SAT plan.

Directions: In the frames below help Carrie move through the four steps of the SAT plan. The first frame shows Carrie reminding herself of the first step of the plan. In the other frames illustrate Carrie and write in her self-talk for that step of the plan. What will be her sensible thinking? Will she lighten up somehow? Will she make a joke about it? What will be her plan? Will she *do* or *say* something that is calm and strong? You decide.

Managing Emotions 7:

Disappointment

Disappointment is part of life. Yet, if an unfortunate event arouses very negative self-talk, disappointment could turn into extreme worry or depression. With some self-discipline, our "thinking brains" can help us manage disappointing events and avoid becoming overly emotional.

Activity

1. With the class discuss the nature of disappointment and some examples of disappointing events.
2. Read to the class the following story about disappointment:

   Juan was excited when he arrived home. This was the day his father was getting a new car. He came into the house and saw his father. "Well," Juan asked, "where's our new wheels?" "Sorry, son," his father said. "I don't think we are going to be able to get a new car until next year." Juan ran up to his room. *This is absolutely horrible*," Juan said to himself. "*This is totally unfair! My old man is nothing but a rotten liar. This is the worst day of my life!*" Juan kicked his door, pounded his fist through his bedroom wall and began swearing at his father.

3. Discuss Juan's reaction with the class. Do his H-B-R on the chalkboard. Be sure to examine his negative beliefs, his unproven, exaggerated statements about not getting the new car.

Stress that the disappointment became *extreme* disappointment because of these thoughts. Juan upset himself by telling himself how awful, terrible, horrible it was that he was disappointed.

---

4. Tell each of the students to work on a blank piece of paper and draw Juan up in his bedroom. He needs help with his self-talk. The students should show Juan using sensible self-talk about the disappointing happening. He can more successfully deal with disappointment by being calm and strong. The finished works can be shared in groups, with the class, or put up on a bulletin board.

Reflection Journal

Direct students to draw pictures of themselves when they experienced some disappointment in life. They should show their self-talk as part of their pictures. Ask them to reflect on these questions: Was your self-talk very exaggerated and extreme? Did it allow your emotional brain to take over? Did you overreact? Or, were you able to think about the disappointment in a balanced, fair way and react in a calm, strong way?

Disappointment

Disappointment is part of life. Still, you don't want your emotional brain to flood your thinking brain with extreme worry or depression. You can show great self-discipline by using the SAT plan to help you manage disappointing events and avoid becoming overly emotional.

SCENARIO: Carlos was ready to leave for the campsite. He had waited all week for this. Then, the phone rang. It was the campground calling. The staff had made a mistake; there were no campsites available. Carlos could not go.

Directions: Carlos was disappointed, naturally. But he decided not to get overly down about all of this. In his mind he went through the four steps of the SAT plan. Help him out: in the frames below use words and illustrations to show how Carlos may have used the SAT plan to manage his disappointment.

SAT Plan

1. Stop. Relax.

2. Think sensibly ... just because ...

3. Make a plan: Be calm, be strong.

4. Reward yourself.

STEP 1	STEP 2
STEP 3	STEP 4

Managing Emotions 8:

Sadness

Sadness is something we will all experience. Yet, none of us will benefit from overreacting to sad events, from being dominated by sadness. We can learn to manage sad events by using the SAT plan: to interrupt negative, unproven self-talk; to think sensibly about what has happened; and to develop a fair, responsible plan of action.

Activity

1. Discuss with the students that we all experience sad events, we will all have sadness in our lives. However, we can learn to manage our own sadness, to avoid letting our emotional brains swamp us, perhaps with feelings of utter worthlessness or depression.

2. Read to the class:

   Twan got his math test back. He failed miserably. He went home and locked himself in his room. *"I am no good,"* he said to himself. *"Everybody will know how stupid I am. Nobody will like me. I am a worthless idiot."*

3. Now, with the class, examine closely Twan's negative, unproven beliefs about having failed the math test. Does failing a math test prove he is no good? Will everybody think he is stupid? Does failing a math test *prove* he is stupid? Will his friends stop liking him? Does failing a math test make Twan "a worthless idiot"? Twan needs the students' help. How could he think about failing a math test in a more balanced, rational way? Tell the students to work in pairs and help Twan by writing up three or four sensible statements about what it really means to fail a math test.

Stress here that Twan's negative, unproven, exaggerated beliefs are actually creating more sadness and depression for him. It is not the sad happening that has deepened his own despair, but the negative view he is rehearsing in his own head.

Reflection Journal

Tell students to illustrate in their journals when they experienced some sadness in life. They should show their self-talk as part of their pictures. Ask them to reflect on these questions: Did your negative self-talk allow your emotional brain to swamp you in depression? Do you think you became *overly* sad? Or, were you able to think about the disappointment in a sensible, balanced way?

Sadness

Sad things happen to everyone. Still, you are not helped by overreacting, or by being dominated by sadness. You can learn to manage sad events by using the SAT plan to avoid negative, unproven self-talk, to think sensibly about what has happened, and to make a calm, strong plan of action. You can exercise self-discipline.

SCENARIO: Lacey really likes a boy in her class, but this boy likes someone else.

Directions: If Lacey came to you for some advice, how would you help her? In the frames below use words and illustrations to show how Lacey might use the SAT plan to help manage her sadness. She will need some sensible ideas for Step 2; she will need a suggestion for a calm, strong plan for Step 3. Lacey appreciates your help!

SAT Plan

1. Stop. Relax.

2. Think sensibly
    ... just because ...

3. Make a plan: Be calm, be strong.

4. Reward yourself.

STEP 1	STEP 2
STEP 3	**STEP 4**

Managing Emotions 9:
Frustration

Frustration is an anxiety that comes from not being able to do what we want to do. From time to time in our lives we will experience frustrating events. This is normal, a part of life. But we can learn to manage our emotional reactions to these events. Our "thinking brains" can prevent our "emotional brains" from flooding us with anxiety. The SAT plan embraces rational thinking and creative solutions to frustrating events.

Activity

1. Explain to the class that frustration is an anxiety they might feel when they are unable to do what they want. For example: Someone is trying to fix a broken clock and just can't get it to work. Ask students to identify some other frustrating situations.
2. Have students role-play characters dealing with frustrating events. Tell half of the groups to show the main character overreacting to the frustrating event; the other half should show the main character managing frustration with sensible self-talk and a responsible plan. In these skits it is important that the characters think out loud. After each skit, point out how the character's self-talk contributed to the reaction.

Reflection Journal

Tell students to draw themselves in the midst of some frustration in life. Remind them to show their self-talk as part of their pictures. Then ask them to do honest, written reflections on these questions: Did your negative self-talk add to the frustration you felt? Do you think you became overly frustrated? Or, were you able to think about the frustrating event in a calm, strong way?

Frustration

Frustrating things do happen! But it is not in anyone's best interest to become overly frustrated. In the face of frustrating events the SAT plan will help you think sensibly about what has happened and come up with a workable, creative solution. Every time you use the SAT plan you are demonstrating emotional intelligence! You are demonstrating self-discipline!

SCENARIO: Scott has jobs to get done before his mom gets home, but he can't find his house keys.

Directions: Scott doesn't want his emotional brain to cause a state of panic inside him. He remembers the SAT plan. In the frames below use words and illustrations to show how Scott might use the SAT plan to avoid panic. Show how calm, sensible thinking will help; show how a good plan will help Scott out of this dilemma.

SAT Plan

1. Stop. Relax.

2. Think sensibly ... just because ...

3. Make a plan: Be calm, be strong.

4. Reward yourself.

STEP 1	STEP 2
STEP 3	STEP 4

Managing Emotions 10:

Anger

Anger is a normal emotion. Nonetheless it is all too often a hairtrigger response that leads to violence. We must learn to discipline our anger. Using the SAT plan, we can allow our "thinking brains" to temper surges from our "emotional brains." We can avoid becoming extremely angry or overly aggressive. Managing anger demonstrates a lot of self-discipline!

Activity

1. Explain to the class that getting angry is normal. Nonetheless, it is important that we learn to control our anger: to become "a little" angry rather than extremely angry. We can learn to deal with unfortunate events without becoming verbally rude and overly aggressive. We can learn to be calm and strong.
2. Have students role-play characters dealing with anger-provoking events. In each skit the actors should show the main character managing anger with sensible self-talk and a responsible plan. Remind the students that the characters should think out loud.
3. Following each skit, applaud the main character's ability to think sensibly about what has happened, to be calm and strong, to have the thinking brain in control.

Remind students of these sensible thinking strategies: (i) to lighten up thoughts (e.g.,This is unfortunate, but it's not the end of the world); (ii) to jump to the right conclusions (e.g., Getting called a name doesn't mean I *am* that name); (iii) to laugh about it (e.g., Yeah, I think these new boots make me look a bit like an alien from outer space).

Reflection Journal

Tell students to think about the last time they became angry about something. In their journals they should do their H-B-Rs. Ask: What self-talk were you going through? Do you think your self-talk was actually contributing to the anger you were feeling? Do you think you could ever substitute funny, or "lighten-up" thoughts to calm down and see the situation differently?

Anger

Anger is a normal human emotion. But anger is all too often a hairtrigger response that leads to violence. Too much anger can turn small problems into bigger problems. You can learn to lighten up when people become annoying. You can learn to see some humor in these situations. Reacting in these ways will make all problems smaller and shows great self-discipline.

SCENARIO: Nicole is talking to her "sweetheart," Louie. Some girls come by, giggle, and start to tease Nicole. Then, they start to tease Louie. The girls are having great fun teasing the two.

Directions: Both Nicole and Louie have a choice: (i) to react angrily to these girls, or (ii) to react in a calm, strong way. In the frames below show how Nicole and Louie avoid angry responses. Be sure to show each person's self-talk!

How does Nicole use sensible thinking to either lighten up or see some humor in this?

What is her plan? What can she say or do?

How does Louie use sensible thinking to either lighten up or see some humor in this?

What is his plan? What can he say or do?

Managing Emotions 11:

Worry

To worry is to be human, but it is important for us not to let our worried states get the best of us. Our emotional brains have the capacity to launch a flood of worry; in fact, we could become swamped with worried thoughts. While we should be *concerned* about many things, the state of worry is often overwhelming and incapacitating. Instead of fretting about an uncertain event, we need to think positively and relax, and create an action plan. That certainly beats worrying!

Activity

1. Explain to the class that you will help them to get worried about a fictitious situation. Have students close their eyes, be quiet, and put their heads down. Tell them to focus only on your words. Read:

   I want you to imagine you are sitting in your room. There is a big math test tomorrow. You say to yourself: *"If I fail this test it will be horrible! My mom will kill me. Everyone will know how stupid I am. It will be the end of the world."* You continue to think about the test. You think about nothing else. You try to open your math book to study, but you cannot study. You can only think about failing that test. You are getting very sad. You can feel a knot in the pit of your stomach. Again you tell yourself: *"I am absolutely stupid at math! Just totally stupid. I should hate myself for being so stupid. I don't see anything I can do about it."*

2. Discuss the simulation briefly. Do a little survey with the students: On a scale of 10 (the most) how worried did you become? What helped you most to get worried?

3. Next, tell the class to co-operate in a second simulation, eyes closed. Read:

   Once again you are sitting in your room. There is a big math test tomorrow. You say to yourself: *"I hope I do well on this test, but if I don't it's really not the end of my life! Mom would be disappointed, but we would both get over it. We always do. My friends wouldn't care if I failed a math test. They might razz me a bit, but that's ok. It's just a little razzing. I'm not as talented in math as I am in other things. That's ok. Everybody has talents and weaknesses. Here is my plan. I am going to study one hour before supper and two hours tonight. I will do the best I can on the test. If I fail, I fail. I'm still a great person."* You then take a moment to become relaxed. You can concentrate on your homework. You are calm, happy, and focused. You can do it!

4. Briefly discuss this simulation. Ask the students: How relaxed did you become? Did you become concerned but not worried about your math test?

Reflection Journal

Direct students to reflect in their journals on one thing that may create some worry for them. Can they describe the beliefs or self-talk that accompanies their worrying? Tell them to write some positive, sensible self-talk that could reduce their stress. Ask: Do you think you could react in a concerned way and avoid a lot of worrying?

Worry

Being concerned about certain events in our lives is healthy. But worrying *excessively* is almost always negative and useless. In fact, if you are flooded with worry, you won't be able to act wisely. Instead of fretting about an uncertain event, you can practise relaxation and positive thinking, and create an action plan. That certainly beats worrying and worrying and worrying!

SCENARIO: Butch has a big math test coming up. He hates math! At first he begins to worry: negative, unproven, exaggerated thoughts fill his head. Worry begins to flood his brain. Worry is taking over!

<u>Directions</u>: Butch needs your help. Using words and illustrations show how Butch can be *concerned* about the math test, yet stop worrying.

STEP ONE: As soon as Butch starts to worry, he should remember the first step of the SAT plan. What does he tell himself? How can he become relaxed?	STEP TWO: How can Butch think sensibly about the math test and also about the possibility of failing the test? "Just because I have a math test ... " and "Even if I fail a test ... "
STEP THREE: Butch needs a calm, strong plan. What is a good plan to get ready for this test? How should he prepare himself for the possibility of not doing well?	STEP FOUR: Butch should congratulate himself for not overreacting! What can he say to himself?

Managing Emotions 12:

Guilt

We have all experienced feelings of guilt. Feeling some remorse at having done something we wish we had not is quite appropriate. Our feelings of remorse may very well help steer our moral behavior. But feeling chronically swamped with guilt is not useful. We can learn to distinguish "chronic guilt" from "honest regret." Further, we can learn to think sensibly about what we have done, make a courageous plan, and move on.

Activity

1. Briefly discuss the concept of guilt. What sort of feeling is guilt? Perhaps someone could look the word up in the class dictionary.

2. Invite the class to consider Daniel's situation. He has been fretting about something for three days now. Read Daniel's story:

   A few days ago Daniel was with some of his classmates in the school hallway. Some of the guys noticed a boy from another class coming down the hall. One of the boys started teasing him: "Hey Daniel, here comes Little Joe. He tried out for the basketball team last night. Man, was he bad!" Daniel began laughing. He then said: "If they had a stepladder he might have made the team." At that they all laughed. After that Daniel regretted his remarks. He said to himself: *"I should never have said those things. I was selfish. I just wanted to get a few laughs from the guys. Now that kid feels rotten. I hate myself. I am unkind, selfish and stupid."*

Suggest to the class that feelings of remorse or regret are quite appropriate, quite healthy. These feelings help us to be decent human beings. These feelings may actually remind us to be kind and responsible, to have empathy for others, to do the right thing. On the other hand, to have our *emotional brains* completely flood us with guilt is often useless. It is healthy to resolve our feelings of regret, to practise *balanced sensible thinking* about what we have done, to have courage, to make a plan, and to move on.

3. Direct students to work in small groups. Each group will need a marker and one piece of chart paper. Explain that Daniel needs some help. He continues to fret away day after day, feeling guilty, stuck in the mud. He needs a SAT plan. Each group should develop a plan for him which suggests some sensible, positive thinking about what he has done and action reflecting calm, strong thinking. Each group should present their four-step SAT plan to the class.

Reflection Journal

Tell students to pretend that they have done something they regret and to describe the situation in their journals. Then, direct them to write a SAT plan which would help them resolve their guilt and move on.

Guilt

It is normal to feel regret or remorse at having done something wrong. Regretting something you've done wrong reminds you to do the right thing next time. But it is not useful to be swamped with guilt. Your thinking brain can help you substitute honest regret for chronic guilt. You can learn to think sensibly about what you have done, make a courageous plan, and move on.

SCENARIO: There were two boys, Damien and Toad. Each did something they would come to regret: shoplifting. Both were caught.

Directions: Read the first frame below. Damien is shown to experience chronic guilt. Day after day he dwells on what he has done wrong. He blames himself over and over. He becomes depressed over his guilt. He doesn't even want to go to school anymore.

On the other hand, Toad refuses to be swamped with chronic guilt. He comes to honestly regret what he has done, forgive himself, and move on. In the second frame do an illustration of Toad. Show his self-talk: give him some honest, sensible thinking about what he has done. He needs two plans: (i) What could he do or say to the shop owner? (ii) What will he do the next time his friends may want to break the law?

SAT Plan

1. Stop. Relax.

2. Think sensibly ... just because ...

3. Make a plan: Be calm, be strong.

4. Reward yourself.

Here is Damien. His negative, exaggerated self-talk is flooding his brain with chronic guilt. Day after day he berates himself for what he has done. Is this useful?

Here is Toad. His balanced thinking allows him to honestly regret what he has done, to make some plans, to get over this, and move on!

I'm a loser. I'll never live this down. I will hate myself forever. I am totally stupid for doing this. I am so rotten. I am NO GOOD. Nobody will ever respect me again! I HATE myself! My parents will KILL me!

UNIT 5

Building Relationships

Take care of each other. Share your energies with
the group. No one must feel alone, cut off — for
that is when you do not make it.

— Willi Unsoeld, mountain climber

Building Relationships

There is little doubt that our ability to build positive relationships will contribute significantly to our overall happiness in life. Building positive relationships links strongly to our capacity to do well in the workforce.

Students build *social intelligence*, or *relationship intelligence*, when they develop a set of "people skills": learning to listen; learning to see the perspectives of others; learning to generate solutions to problems. In this section students will learn and practise the Win-Win plan — a three-step plan for solving relationship problems.

Also, building relationships has much to do with character: respecting others, being kind, showing patience, possessing the courage to act on our own values. These characteristics are the essence of self-discipline.

	SUMMARY OF BUILDING RELATIONSHIPS SESSIONS	
1	ACTIVE LISTENING	Active listening as more than simply listening
2	SEEING ANOTHER'S POINT OF VIEW	Building healthy relationships is linked to our ability to see others' perspectives.
3	CREATING POSSIBILITIES	Learning to think divergently, to create possible options to social problems
4	WIN-WIN POSSIBILITIES	I win–you win: Raising our Relationship I.Q.
5	THE WIN-WIN PLAN	The Win-Win Plan: An alternative to arguing and fighting!
6	COACH BOB & THE WIN-WIN PLAN	The Win-Win Plan: Social problem solving with adults
7	MOM, SATURDAY NIGHT & THE WIN-WIN PLAN	The Win-Win Plan: Social problem solving with parents
8	FRIDAY NIGHT, FRIENDS & THE WIN-WIN PLAN	The Win-Win Plan: Social problem solving with friends
9	MAKING THE PROBLEM SMALLER	Saying the right things, doing the right things makes every problem smaller
10	SHOWING PATIENCE	Learning to build positive relationships by practising patience
11	HAVING COURAGE	Learning to build positive relationships by practising courage

Building Relationships 1:
Active Listening

Active listening is more than just listening. It provides feedback to the other person; it invites clarification; it shows respect. Listening to someone actively and honestly is an important step in building positive relationships. If we learn to be better active listeners, we can communicate with friends, adults, and others more effectively. We have then raised our relationship intelligence and demonstrated self-discipline.

Activity

1. Initiate a class discussion on the question: Should girls be allowed to join boys' sports teams? Explain that the discussion will follow certain rules:

   (i) One person speaks at a time. To signal you would like to speak, put your hand up. The teacher will act as mediator.

   (ii) All sincere opinions are welcome.

   (iii) Before offering an opinion, you must rephrase the last person's comments (e.g., Cheryl made the point that boys are not necessarily stronger than girls).

Such a discussion should be lively and fun; it should also ensure effective listening. You might make the active listening rules apply to the classroom discussions or debates. The students will become better at this with practice.

Stress here that providing feedback to someone really demonstrates that you have listened to that person. When you rephrase what someone has just said, you are winning respect from that person. You have increased your chances of that person really listening to you.

Reflection Journal

Direct students to think of someone in their lives who seems to really listen to them. Ask them to reflect on this person in their journals: In what ways does this person show he/she is a good listener? Might good listening be a social intelligence?

Active Listening

Active listening is more than just listening. You are demonstrating active listening when you occasionally give feedback to a speaker, when you communicate that you are hearing that person, that you really understand what that person is saying. If you learn to listen actively, you have increased your ability to communicate. You have raised your relationship intelligence! You have shown self-discipline!

SCENARIO: Jake has just found out that his parents are getting a divorce. On Saturday he comes over to David's house.

Directions: In the space below finish the discussion that David and Jake are having about Jake's sad situation. Your writing of this discussion should show that David is a good friend, that he cares, that he listens actively.

David: So when did you find out?

Jake: It's been going on for a while, probably a year or so ... I guess the first time I heard them talk about it was last year. They were arguing a lot.

David: I guess you're pretty mixed up or scared right now, hey?

Building Relationships 2:
Seeing Another's Point of View

Seeing another's point of view is not always easy. When we were very young it was difficult for us to see another perspective, to understand how someone else thought and felt about certain things. As we grow older it becomes increasingly important that we appreciate another's point of view. It is a social skill friends, classmates, and adults expect. Fortunately, seeing another's point of view is something we can learn. If we practise doing this actively, we will be showing an important relationship skill. And we will be showing self-discipline.

Activity

1. Have a brief class discussion about the difficulty (sometimes) of seeing another person's point of view. Suggest to the class that trying to understand how other people see and feel about things is a social intelligence that should strengthen with age; it is much easier for a twelve-year-old to see different perspectives than it is for a three-year-old.
2. Present to the class the following scenario: A son or daughter wants to stay out late on Saturday night. The parent disagrees.
3. Working in pairs, one student should take the role of the parent, the other the son or daughter. Let them play out the discussion. After about 10 minutes, instruct each pair to have the same discussion — but this time to reverse roles.
4. On chart paper or chalkboard create two columns: Parent and Son/Daughter. With the entire class list the concerns/thoughts/feelings that were central to the parent in their discussions. Then, list the concerns/thoughts/feelings that were important for the son or daughter.

Suggest that if students are going to form good relationships with adults, friends, and acquaintances, it will be important for them to see another point of view. It sometimes takes time, patience, and effort, but they will be smarter socially!

Reflection Journal

Instruct students to think about one area of disagreement they may have with someone in their lives. Now, for the reflection, tell them to take that other person's point of view and make a reflection based on it.

Seeing Another's Point of View

It is not always easy to see someone else's perspective, or point of view. But it is important! As you actively practise seeing another's viewpoint, as you get better at seeing how someone else is seeing something, you improve your relationship intelligence.

SCENARIO: Gracie wants to have a party Saturday. Mom says no. To understand Gracie's point of view read what she is thinking here:

"Janice had a party last month. Rachel had a party before that! I just want to be fair and do my part in the friendship. If I don't invite them to something, they might think I don't like them, or that I'm not doing my turn. We're not going to create a mess or anything. We won't make a big disturbance. We're just going to rent a video and have some fun. I really don't understand why Mom is so pigheaded about this! I just don't understand!"

<u>Directions</u>: Help Gracie to understand her mom's point of view. In the space below (a) draw Gracie's mom, and then (b) write her thoughts, her reasons for not allowing Gracie to have the girls over on Saturday. It will be interesting to see her point of view!

Building Relationships 3:
Creating Possibilities

Creating possibilities is an important relationship intelligence for all of us. Much of the dynamics within relationships is a kind of social problem solving. If we are able to see only one choice, one possible solution to a problem we are having with someone, we are stuck! We will be smarter socially if we can see different possibilities for solving our problems.

Activity

1. Tell the students to work in pairs. Each pair will need a pen and paper. Remind students of the staying-out-late issue discussed in the previous session. In that session a teenager wanted to stay out late on Saturday night but the parent disagreed with that.
2. Ask each pair to make a list of at least three suggestions that might solve the problem for the parent and teenager. What possibilities might be agreeable to both the teenager and the parent?
3. Have each pair share their possibilities with the class.

Stress that it is important, first of all, to try to understand the point of view of others. Why does the parent not want the teenager to stay out late? How is the parent feeling and thinking? Secondly, the ability to suggest different possibilities that might be agreeable to both sides often helps a relationship to become "unstuck."

Reflection Journal

Direct students to reflect once again on the area of disagreement on which they wrote last time. For their written reflection, tell them to create several possibilities that might solve the disagreement, possibilities which might be agreeable to both them and the other person.

Creating Possibilities

You are involved in social problem solving nearly every day: with friends, classmates, parents, adults. If you see only one answer, one possibility to solving a problem, you are stuck! On the other hand, you show a lot of social intelligence if you can suggest several possibilities to a problem. You will be more effective with people if you are able to see possibilities and create options.

SCENARIO: Trinny, Reena, and Mark are all in the same class at school, and each of them is experiencing a problem with a relationship. They need your help!

<u>Directions</u>: Read each problem and write three possible solutions for it.

PROBLEM

Trinny's parents have a camping vacation planned for summer. Trinny would rather stay home and play minor baseball. He dreams of being a pro someday.

SOLUTION 1:

SOLUTION 2:

SOLUTION 3:

PROBLEM

Reena just got her driver's licence. She wants the car this Friday night. It's a very special night! Older brother Jimmie also wants the car for a very big night!

SOLUTION 1:

SOLUTION 2:

SOLUTION 3:

PROBLEM

Mark's bike has a flat. He has got to get to the gym for basketball practice. Should he take his sister's bike without asking? They have an agreement: if you borrow, ask first!

SOLUTION 1:

SOLUTION 2:

SOLUTION 3:

Building Relationships 4:
Win-Win Possibilities

"Win-Win Possibilities" is an exercise in social problem solving. Not too surprisingly, many social conflicts end with someone winning, someone losing. In fact, many of us work towards that from the beginning of the conflict: I win–you lose. However, we demonstrate more emotional maturity if we can suggest "I win–you win" possibilities to a difficulty we are having. This approach isn't always easy. It takes courage! And it takes self-discipline.

Activity

1. On chart paper or chalkboard present to students the following grid.

I LOSE –YOU LOSE
I LOSE –YOU WIN
I WIN–YOU LOSE
I WIN–YOU WIN

Suggest that all social squabbles, disagreements, and conflicts have possible outcomes in terms of winning and losing. Discuss the four possibilities on this grid. What are some examples of each one? If someone is in a disagreement with someone, what is their position, their hope most likely to be? Which outcome is ideal?

2. Ask the students to work in groups. A recorder will need pen and paper. Each group should design a conflict (e.g., two sisters wanting to watch different T.V. shows), and then write one example for each of the four possibilities.

Example: It is Monday night. I want to watch my television show. My sister comes in. She really wants to watch her show.	I LOSE–YOU LOSE	We get in a big fight. Mom turns off the television.
	I LOSE –YOU WIN	I let her have her way. I storm off and sulk in my room.
	I WIN–YOU LOSE	I overpower her. She goes off and sulks in her room.
	I WIN–YOU WIN	We agree upon television times for her and for me.

Allow the groups to present their four possibilities. Make the point that win-win solutions are sometimes difficult. In terms of the SAT plan, the Win-Win plan is a way of being calm and strong. It takes courage, patience, and strength to agree to I win–you win solutions.

Reflection Journal

Instruct students to create in their journals a win-win possibility to a real-life conflict that may happen (or may be happening) in their lives.

Win-Win Possibilities

Imagine that you and I have a disagreement. Now look at the chart to the right. This chart suggests four types of solutions to the problem. Not too surprisingly, many conflicts end with someone winning, someone losing. You show more emotional intelligence if you are able to suggest "I win–you win" possibilities to resolve a disagreement. This takes imagination. It takes courage! And it takes self-discipline.

| I LOSE–YOU LOSE |
| I LOSE–YOU WIN |
| I WIN–YOU LOSE |
| I WIN–YOU WIN |

SCENARIO: Michael and Bruno have decided to set up their own environmental club. Michael thinks *he* will make the best leader for the club; he wants to be president. Bruno thinks *he* will make the best leader; he wants to be president.

<u>Directions</u>: In the space provided write one example of each of the four types of solutions.

PROBLEM	I LOSE–YOU LOSE
Who should be president of the environmental club?	I LOSE–YOU WIN
	I WIN–YOU LOSE
	I WIN–YOU WIN

Illustrate your Win-Win possibility.

Building Relationships 5:
The Win-Win Plan

The Win-Win plan is a neat, three-step guideline for virtually any social conflict. Learning to create win-win possibilities elevates our social intelligence. Agreeing to a win-win solution allows us to be calm and strong; it shows emotional maturity, courage, and self-discipline. We should remember to congratulate ourselves for even trying to solve problems with a win-win approach.

Activity

1. On chart paper present to students the three-step Win-Win plan. *Suggestion*: Keep the plan in a conspicuous place in the room as a permanent reference. Use it often! Review the three steps of the Win-Win plan. Remember that active listening is more than simply listening. It involves honest listening as well as communicating that you are listening. Stating your thoughts or feelings calmly is a way of being calm and strong. For example: "There are three shows on tonight that I really don't want to miss. But I am willing to be fair about this." Suggest a win-win possibility. (For example: "I have a suggestion: Let's work out a television-watching schedule. How can we do this?")

> **The Win-Win Plan**
> 1. Listen actively to the other person.
> 2. State your thoughts or feelings calmly.
> 3. Suggest a win-win possibility.

2. Display the problem scenarios, outlined at right, on the chalkboard. Let pairs of students select one problem scenario. Have one person act as the leader in working through the Win-Win plan.

3. Ask students to take turns using the Win-Win plan to solve the problems.

> **Problem Scenarios**
> 1. Mom wants you to do homework right after school; you want to play soccer.
> 2. Your brother keeps coming into your room; you want more privacy.
> 3. Mom wants you to get a job on Saturday night; you want to party with friends.
> 4. You want to see your movie; your friend wants another.

Reflection Journal

Instruct students to use the Win-Win plan in a real-life situation. Tell them to record in their journals their personal reflections on how the experiment went.

The Win-Win Plan

The Win-Win plan is an alternative to arguing and fighting. Agreeing to win-win solutions allows you to be calm and strong. It shows emotional intelligence, maturity, and courage. It shows self-discipline.

SCENARIO: Jazzy and her friends are at the park playing basketball. Then, some other kids start to play in the same area. There is nearly a fight! Jazzy decides that arguing and fighting make problems worse. She takes some leadership and tries the Win-Win plan.

Directions: Complete the story sequence below with illustrations and text. Show how Jazzy successfully uses the Win-Win plan to avoid a big fight.

> **The Win-Win Plan**
> 1. Listen actively to the other person.
> 2. State your thoughts or feelings calmly.
> 3. Suggest a win-win possibility.

1. Other kids start playing in the same area. Jazzy's friends begin taunting them. Things are heating up!	2. Jazzy decides to take some leadership. She remembers the three steps of the Win-Win plan.
3. Step One: She gets the other kids' side of the story and listens actively. She rephrases what the kids have said to show that she understands and respects their point of view.	4. Step Two: She calmly states her thoughts.
5. Step Three: She suggests a win-win possibility.	6. It works!

Building Relationships 6:

Coach Bob & the Win-Win Plan

"Coach Bob & the Win-Win Plan" is a simulation allowing students to practise social problem solving with adults. The more comfortable we become with the Win-Win plan, the more likely it is that we will use it. The Win-Win plan is our alternative to sulking, fretting, arguing. It allows each of us to be "a doer, not a stewer."

Activity

1. Review the Win-Win plan with students. See if some can state the three steps without looking at it. Ask: How does listening actively differ from simply listening? (You give feedback; you rephrase what someone said.)

2. Have students work in pairs for the Coach Bob simulation. This activity will give them an opportunity to practise social problem solving with an adult. Outline this scenario: You are on a baseball team. Coach Bob is quite strict. He has put you in left field for the first three games of the season. Yet, you want to try catching. Once, you meekly mentioned this at a practice, but he did not seem to listen. You decide to see him privately after practice and introduce a win-win plan.

3. Tell students to practise their simulations in pairs for several minutes. Then, have several of the pairs do their simulations in front of the class. Make points about eye contact, body posture, tone of voice: body language can be significant!

> The Win-Win Plan
> 1. Listen actively to the other person.
> 2. State your thoughts or feelings calmly.
> 3. Suggest a win-win possibility.

Stress that it takes great courage to come forward and act on our interests! This may be especially true for students dealing with adults. Students should be proud of themselves for even *attempting* to stick up for themselves in a responsible, respectful, yet assertive way! A win-win agreement is not always reached, but the attempt to reach it shows that someone has been calm and strong — "a doer, not a stewer."

Reflection Journal

Direct students to think back about whether there has ever been an adult other than a parent with whom they might have used the Win-Win plan. The adult might be a coach, teacher, or neighbor. How could the plan have gone? Could it have worked out? Tell students to reflect in their journals.

Coach Bob & the Win-Win Plan

The more comfortable you become in using the Win-Win plan, the more likely you will use it, even with adults in your life. The Win-Win plan is your alternative to sulking, fretting, arguing. You can learn to be "a doer, not a stewer."

SCENARIO: What should Ian do? Coach Bob seems to be yelling at him in class, picking on him. Ian decides that there is little gain in simply stewing about the situation. He asks to see Coach Bob after school so he can try the win-win approach.

> **The Win-Win Plan**
> 1. Listen actively to the other person.
> 2. State your thoughts or feelings calmly.
> 3. Suggest a win-win possibility.

<u>Directions</u>: Complete the story sequence below with illustrations and text. What will Ian say to move through the steps of the Win-Win plan?

1. Coach Bob seems to be picking on Ian. 	2. Ian is a little nervous but he makes an appointment to see Coach Bob after class.
3. Step One: Ian asks Coach Bob if there's a problem. He listens actively, occasionally rephrasing what Coach Bob has said, showing respect and understanding.	4. Step Two: Ian calmly states his feelings.
5. Step Three: Ian suggests a win-win possibility.	6. The next day in class

Building Relationships 7:
Mom, Saturday & the Win-Win Plan

"Mom, Saturday & the Win-Win Plan" is another simulation in forming win-win solutions: this time with a parent. Students are more likely to have an "argument" with a parent if they consider only their own wants: I win–you lose. But if they are able to actively listen to the parent, and communicate that they hear and understand the parent's concerns and that they respect those concerns, then they might work out a win-win agreement with the parent.

Activity

1. Review the Win-Win plan with students. A win-win solution is one possibility. What are the other three? (I win–you lose; I lose–you win; I lose–you lose).

2. Have students work in pairs for a Saturday night simulation. They will have an opportunity to practise social problem solving with a parent. Here is their scenario: There is a party at Janine's on Saturday night and you are dying to go. But you know your mom will have some concerns about this party; she probably won't let you go. You decide to sit down with her and try to come up with a win-win proposition.

3. Tell students to practise their simulations in pairs for several minutes. Ask several of the pairs to do their simulations for the class. The students should observe and comment on eye contact, body posture, and tone of voice.

> **The Win-Win Plan**
> 1. Listen actively to the other person.
> 2. State your thoughts or feelings calmly.
> 3. Suggest a win-win possibility.

Stress that arguments are rarely productive. That's because they are usually characterized by I win–you lose approaches by both people. Students are more likely to work out agreements with their parents if they actively listen, state their interests respectfully, and work towards a solution that satisfies all concerns. This process takes patience and courage, and it won't always work perfectly!

Reflection Journal

Instruct students to think of some issue they can work out with their mom or dad. Each of them should make an appointment with a parent and go through the three steps of the Win-Win plan. In their journals, they should reflect on the process. How did it go? How did they feel about it?

Mom, Saturday & the Win-Win Plan

You are more likely to have an argument with a parent if you consider only your own wants: I win–you lose. But if you are able to listen actively to your parent, and communicate that you hear and understand the other point of view, then you might work out a win-win arrangement.

SCENARIO: Callie needs some help. Her mom wants her to do her homework on Saturday morning. But Callie wants to catch her favorite T.V. show at that time.

Directions: Complete the illustrations and dialogue in the story sequence below as Callie works through the Win-Win plan with her mom.

The Win-Win Plan
1. Listen actively to the other person.
2. State your thoughts or feelings calmly.
3. Suggest a win-win possibility.

Callie doesn't understand why her mom is so pig-headed. The more Callie thinks about it, the more furious she becomes.	Home work on Saturday Morning! That's ridiculous! I can't believe Mom is so pigheaded! I could just SCREAM!
Callie calms down. She tells herself to stop, relax. She has an idea: the Win-Win plan.	
Step One: She actively listens to her mom's point of view. She rephrases, shows respect.	
Step Two: Callie states her feelings.	
Step Three: Callie suggests a win-win possibility.	
Here is what happened.	

Building Relationships 8:

Friday Night, Friends & the Win-Win Plan

"Friday Night, Friends & the Win-Win Plan" is another simulation in forming win-win solutions: this time within a group of friends. What would happen if friends got together on Friday night and each had a different notion of what to do? Would they argue? Would they fight? Or can they use the Win-Win plan?

Activity

1. Review again the Win-Win plan with students. If it is covered up, can they remember the three steps?

2. For this simulation students should work in small groups. Each group should plan a short skit to act out in front of the class. Here is the scenario: You are a group of friends getting ready to go out on a Friday night. But different people want to do different things. It seems that there is going to be an argument. Can you somehow work through a Win-Win plan?

The Win-Win Plan
1. Listen actively to the other person.
2. State your thoughts or feelings calmly.
3. Suggest a win-win possibility.

3. Encourage the audience to listen carefully for the three steps of the plan. Ask students to consider these questions: Did everyone in the group actively listen to each other? Could each one state his/her feelings calmly? Did a win-win possibility emerge? Did everyone agree to accept a win-win possibility? What would happen if someone refused to go along with any win-win agreement?

Reflection Journal

Tell students to think of one problem solving area involving a group of friends. Ask them to state this in their journals, then write personal reflections. Do they think a Win-Win plan could ever work in a group? Would everyone listen to each other? Would everyone agree? What might happen if most friends agreed to a solution, but someone did not?

Friday Night, Friends & the Win-Win Plan

What happens when good friends disagree? Do you argue? Do you fight? Do you sulk? If each of you is willing to be a little patient, to respect another's point of view, then you might work out a win-win agreement. You will have shown much social intelligence.

SCENARIO: It is Friday night. Nate and his friends get together. There is a disagreement.

The Win-Win Plan
1. Listen actively to the other person.
2. State your thoughts or feelings calmly.
3. Suggest a win-win possibility.

Directions: In the frame below use pictures and words to create a story line for Nate and his friends. What will be their problem? How will they move to a Win-Win plan? Will it work?

It is Friday night. Nate and his friends get together. Here is the problem.	
First they listen to each other's point of view.	
Each friend states his own opinion.	
Here is what they decide to do.	
That night	

Building Relationships 9:
Making the Problem Smaller

Making the problem smaller is an important strategy for all social conflicts. For every argument, for every conflict, we must decide whether to make the problem bigger or smaller. With each conflict, then, it helps to ask: "How can I make the problem smaller?"

Activity

1. To begin the class discussion blow up a balloon. Suggest that balloons are somewhat like difficulties we have with other people: some difficulties are small (balloon is small); some are medium (blow some air); and some are large (add more air).
2. Have students work in pairs. Each pair will need pen and paper. Ask students to consider this scenario: Billy notices that his sister, Sarah, has gone into his room without permission. He has told her to stay out of his room!
3. Each pair should draw three balloons on the paper, with the problem identified on the middle balloon. The balloon to the left is drawn smaller: What could Billy do or say to make the problem smaller? The balloon to the right is drawn bigger: What might he do or say that would worsen his problem?
4. Ask students to share some of the results.

Suggest to the students that the balloon is an important reminder of the value of making any problem smaller. When we become upset with someone, we may be tempted to explode or try to get even. This rarely solves our problem.

Reflection Journal

Tell students to think of one area of difficulty they have had with someone. In their reflection journals they should draw three balloons. On the first, have them note the problem, which would stay the same if they did nothing about it. On the smaller balloon, have them note what they could have done to make the problem smaller. And on the bigger balloon, have them note what they might have done to make the problem bigger. Ask them to record what they did do, too.

Making the Problem Smaller

For every argument, for every conflict, you have a choice: (a) you can say or do things to make the problem bigger; (b) you can say or do things to make the problem smaller. With each conflict, then, you are demonstrating social intelligence if you ask yourself: "*How can I make this problem smaller?*"

SCENARIO: Tina is sitting in the school cafeteria. Suddenly a Grade 9 student trips and spills chocolate milk all over Tina. Everybody laughs.

Directions: Use words and pictures to show what Tina might do or say to make this problem bigger, and what she might do or say to make the problem smaller.

Here is how Tina might make her problem bigger.

Here is how Tina might make her problem smaller.

Building Relationships 10:
Showing Patience

Showing patience builds positive relationships. Almost all emotional overreactions are linked to a loss of patience. Our emotional brains have little patience; strong emotions may prompt us to act before we think, to act without patience. Our thinking brains can help: we can learn to calm down before we do or say anything. We can learn to be patient in relationship issues.

Activity

1. Read to the class the story of Frannie and Brian:

   Frannie found out she was not invited to play basketball with the girls on Saturday. Immediately she got on the phone. She phoned Tara. "Hey, you girls are real jerks!" she yelled. "The next time you need an extra player, forget it!" She then slammed down the phone.

   Brian found out that he was not invited to the boys' basketball game on Saturday. He was quite disappointed. He wondered why they hadn't called. "*Oh well,*" he said to himself, "*Be patient. Things will work out. This will pass.*"

2. Discuss: What self-talk helped Brian to be patient? What self-talk helped Frannie to lose patience, to overreact?
3. Direct students to work in small groups. Each group should plan and present a skit: something unfortunate has happened to one of the characters. That character should use positive self-talk to be patient in the situation.

Suggest to the students that having patience is a type of social and emotional maturity. Our emotional brains often prompt us to act without thinking, without patience. But our thinking brains can remind us to be patient. What are some effective statements we can make to help us to be patient with friends, family, others?

Reflection Journal

Instruct students to think of one relationship issue for which they would have liked more patience. Tell them to reflect in their journals on this: What is the issue? What do you think prompted you to have little patience in this situation? How do you think you could become more patient in these times? Do you think someone can learn to become more patient?

Showing Patience

It is not always easy to be patient — it requires self-discipline. But having patience builds positive relationships. Almost all emotional overreactions are linked to a loss of patience. Your emotional brain has little patience, but your thinking brain can help. Using positive self-talk you can learn to calm down before you do or say anything. Learning to be patient adds to your relationship intelligence.

SCENARIO: Most of the time Frannie shows little patience, while Brian does exercise patience. What would happen if Frannie and Brian lost something important to each of them? Do you think their self-talk would differ? How would each of them react?

Directions: First, decide what the characters lost. Then, in the space below, illustrate the reactions of Frannie and Brian, and be sure to show their self-talk. Remember: positive self-talk usually leads to appropriate reactions and negative self-talk, to overreactions!

FRANNIE'S IMPATIENT REACTION	BRIAN'S PATIENT REACTION

Building Relationships 11:

Having Courage

Having courage is important to everyone. But acting on our personal values is not always easy. Nor is it always easy to stick up for ourselves or to say "No." We can learn to have courage, to act on our own values, by reminding ourselves to be calm and strong or to do the right thing!

Activity

1. Read Randy's story:

   Randy went out with some friends on Tuesday night. Finally Chip said: "Hey guys, let's go over to the school and throw some rocks through the windows. It'll be a riot." Some of the others laughed. Randy felt uneasy. It wasn't his thing. He believed it was wrong and stupid, yet his friends were important to him. He said to himself: *Be calm, be strong. I have to have some courage here.*" He looked at Chip, straight in the eye: "Sorry guys, that's a bit stupid. I'm not up for that." Chip became offended: "Are you saying we're stupid, Randy?" "No," Randy replied. "You guys are great, but that idea is a bit stupid. Breaking windows costs my parents and your parents money. Your taxes, my taxes. I'm not up for it. I'll see you guys tomorrow." Randy smiled, turned, and walked away.

2. Have a brief discussion about Randy. What did he tell himself in order to act with courage? Is it harder to be courageous with friends or non-friends?

3. Ask students to work in small groups to plan and present a skit. They should show a character in the skit acting with courage. These characters think out loud to share courageous self-talk.

Make the point that it is often difficult to act with courage, especially with friends. But, in the long run, people respect courageous individuals. Stress too that courageous action comes from courageous self-talk. Ask: What are some courageous self-statements we might use?

Reflection Journal

Invite students to reflect in their journals on a time when they acted with courage. Have them describe the situation and their courageous self-talk. Ask them how they felt afterwards. Were they proud of themselves?

Having Courage

It is not always easy to act on your personal values. It is not always easy to stick up for yourself. And it is not always easy to say "No." You can practise acting with courage on your own values and sticking up for yourself. Just remind yourself to have courage, be calm, be strong, and do the right thing.

SCENARIO: On Saturday Randy went to the park with Matt and Sluggo. At the park Matt and Sluggo noticed a smaller kid playing by himself and they began teasing him. The kid tried to ignore Matt and Sluggo, but the two boys kept taunting him. He was clearly becoming frustrated.

Directions: How should Randy handle this? His friends are important to him, yet he doesn't believe their bullying is right. In the three frames below show (a) Randy's courageous self-talk, (b) what he decides to say and do, and (c) the outcome of his being courageous.

Randy's self-talk

Randy acts.

The outcome

UNIT 6

Living Proof of Growth

You only grow by coming to the end of something
and by beginning something else.

— John Irving,
   American writer

Living Proof of Growth

At the same time as students are developing living skills, they are focusing on personal growth.

Use of a Living Proof portfolio, as explained in Unit 2, will help students create a focus for growing and acquiring self-discipline — for developing a deeper self-awareness, for managing negative emotions better, for building positive social relationships. Each portfolio is personal, unique: it allows the student to commit to personal growth goals and to document strides towards reaching those goals — to provide "living proof" of growth.

SUMMARY OF PORTFOLIO GROWTH SHEETS		
#	Title	How to Use
1	DEVELOPING SELF-AWARENESS Reflections	Ask students to complete this sheet before and after Unit 3. Comparing responses is a type of reflection, one way of thinking about possible growth in hte area of self-awareness.
2	MANAGING EMOTIONS Reflections	Ask students to complete this sheet before and after Unit 4. Did the responses differ? What might this mean?
3	BUILDING RELATIONSHIPS Reflections	Ask students to complete this sheet before and after Unit 5. Which responses changed? Which didn't? What might that suggest?
4	DEVELOPING SELF-AWARENESS Growth, Reflection, Conference	Here the student is encouraged to set a personal goal related to self-awareness, to note proof of growth, to reflect in writing, and to comment on a conference.
5	MANAGING EMOTIONS Growth, Reflection, Conference	The student sets a personal goal related to managing emotions and enters reflections, proofs of growth, and conference notes.
6	BUILDING RELATIONSHIPS Growth, Reflection, Conference	The student sets goals related to building relationships, then enters related reflections, proofs of growth, and conference notes.

DEVELOPING SELF-AWARENESS

Reflections

DIRECTIONS: Before beginning work on the unit Developing Self-Awareness, complete this checklist. Reflect on each statement: How true is it for *you*? Check (✔) your response. Be honest! Once you finish the unit, take time to complete this checklist again.

Items Related to Interest and Awareness

	VERY TRUE	FAIRLY TRUE	A LITTLE TRUE	NOT TRUE
1. I have a keen interest in and curiosity about my own emotions.				
2. I have a keen interest in and curiosity about other people's emotions.				
3. I have a sound knowledge about emotions.				
4. My vocabulary relating to emotions is excellent. I can identify and label most emotions.				
5. I know quite a bit about body language: what it is and how effective it is in communication.				
6. I am aware of my own body language and how effective it is in different social situations.				
7. I appreciate my own body language; I think about it, pay attention to it.				
8. I understand quite well how our attitudes, beliefs, self-talk relate to our feelings.				
9. I have a real interest in and appreciation of how my own self-talk affects my emotions.				
10. I try to pay attention to my own attitudes, my self-talk.				
11. I understand quite well how emotional overreactions happen.				
12. I have a real awareness of how my reactions to something relate to what I am telling myself.				
13. I have an interest, a curiosity about how the brain works.				
14. I understand what is happening in the brain when emotions are triggered.				
15. I am quite curious about and interested in learning more about emotions and behavior.				

MANAGING EMOTIONS

Reflections

DIRECTIONS: Before beginning work on the unit Managing Emotions, complete this checklist. Reflect on each statement: How true is it for *you*? Check (✔) your response. Be honest! Once you finish the unit, take time to complete this checklist again.

Items Relating to Interest and Skills

	VERY TRUE	FAIRLY TRUE	A LITTLE TRUE	NOT TRUE
1. I am interested in learning more about relaxation techniques: how to relax deeply.				
2. I understand the techniques of relaxation; I am very good at relaxing my entire body.				
3. I have an interest in how certain attitudes and self-talk might cause personal troubles.				
4. I have a good understanding of how negative self-talk might cause personal troubles.				
5. I have a plan I often use in order to help me avoid overreacting to things that happen to me.				
6. I think I can manage my own disappointment quite well.				
7. I think I can manage my own sadness quite well.				
8. I think I can manage my own frustration quite well.				
9. I think I can manage my own anger quite well.				
10. I think I can manage my own worry quite well.				
11. I think I can manage my own feelings of remorse or guilt quite well.				
12. I often tell myself to lighten up about troubling events.				
13. I often use a sense of humor to avoid becoming overly angry or worried.				
14. If I heard a rumor about myself, I would check it out; I wouldn't jump to conclusions.				
15. I am interested in learning more about avoiding overreactions to unfortunate events.				

BUILDING RELATIONSHIPS

Reflections

DIRECTIONS: Before beginning work on the unit Building Relationships, complete this checklist. Reflect on each statement: How true is it for *you*? Check (✔) your response. Be honest! Once you finish the unit, take time to complete this checklist again.

Items Relating to Interest and Skills

	VERY TRUE	FAIRLY TRUE	A LITTLE TRUE	NOT TRUE
1. I consider myself a good listener in the company of adults.				
2. I consider myself a good listener in the company of my friends.				
3. I have an interest in improving my listening skills.				
4. I think I am quite good at working out fair solutions in disagreements with friends.				
5. I think I am quite good at working out fair solutions in disagreements with adults.				
6. When I am in disagreements with people, I usually try to work out win-win solutions.				
7. I feel quite comfortable in acting assertively with adults.				
8. I feel quite comfortable in acting assertively with friends.				
9. When I have a relationship problem, I usually find a way to make the problem smaller.				
10. I understand the difference between assertiveness and aggressiveness.				
11. I think I show a lot of patience in my relationships with others.				
12. I would like to become more patient in my relationships with others.				
13. I think I have a lot of courage in my relationships with others.				
14. I would like to become more courageous in my relationships with others.				
15. If I heard a rumor about myself, I would check it out; I wouldn't jump to conclusions.				

DEVELOPING SELF-AWARENESS

Growth, Reflection, Conference

Right now my goal in developing self-awareness is . . .

Living Proof of My Growth, My Improvement

Date:_____ *Proof of Growth:*	*My Reflection:*	*Conferenced with:*_____ *Date:*_____ *Comment:*
Date:_____ *Proof of Growth:*	*My Reflection:*	*Conferenced with:*_____ *Date:*_____ *Comment:*
Date:_____ *Proof of Growth:*	*My Reflection:*	*Conferenced with:*_____ *Date:*_____ *Comment:*
Date:_____ *Proof of Growth:*	*My Reflection:*	*Conferenced with:*_____ *Date:*_____ *Comment:*

MANAGING EMOTIONS

Growth, Reflection, Conference

Right now my goal in managing emotions is . . .

Living Proof of My Growth, My Improvement

Date:_____ Proof of Growth:	My Reflection:	Conferenced with:_____ Date:_____ Comment:
Date:_____ Proof of Growth:	My Reflection:	Conferenced with:_____ Date:_____ Comment:
Date:_____ Proof of Growth:	My Reflection:	Conferenced with:_____ Date:_____ Comment:
Date:_____ Proof of Growth:	My Reflection:	Conferenced with:_____ Date:_____ Comment:

BUILDING RELATIONSHIPS

Growth, Reflection, Conference

Right now my goal in building relationships is . . .

Living Proof of My Growth, My Improvement

Date:_____ Proof of Growth:	My Reflection:	Conferenced with:_____ Date:_____ Comment:
Date:_____ Proof of Growth:	My Reflection:	Conferenced with:_____ Date:_____ Comment:
Date:_____ Proof of Growth:	My Reflection:	Conferenced with:_____ Date:_____ Comment:
Date:_____ Proof of Growth:	My Reflection:	Conferenced with:_____ Date:_____ Comment:

The Special Role of Portfolios

It is not the job of teachers to tell students how they must grow, nor is it our job to tell them what is important in their lives. Just as each snowflake is unique, so is each student. Each student portfolio will reflect the uniqueness of its owner: it will be different from all other portfolios, as it should be.

The Living Proof sheets in Unit 6 serve as a framework for students' growth. They also serve as guides for putting students in charge of their own learning, their own self-discipline. Throughout the program young people are gradually developing a deeper awareness of themselves. They are learning about their emotions, especially about managing negative feelings better. They are learning to explore friendships and build relationships. And finally, they are given opportunities to apply their learning to portfolios.

The Living Skills portfolio is a focus for growth, an opportunity to reflect on where students are and how they might get where they need to go. It is another step on the road to students' own self-discipline.

Suggestions for Conferencing

Three Things to Remember About Conferencing

1. A portfolio conference is important! It is an open, honest conversation about the portfolio.

2. Everyone's portfolio is special and unique; therefore, no two portfolios will be the same. Conferences will help another person to understand you; they will help you to understand someone else.

3. Conferences can be done with a classmate, a teacher, a parent; in one-to-one situations or in groups.

Suggestions for Sharing Your Portfolio

1. Talk about how you have organized your portfolio. Why did you do it this way?

2. Talk about the goals you have set for yourself. Why did you select these goals? Why were they important to you?

3. Talk about the things you have done to achieve your goals. What is the "living proof" of your growth, your improvement?

4. Show pieces that make you feel proud. Tell why you included these pieces in your portfolio.

5. Talk about other goals you have been thinking about. Why are these goals important to you?

6. Ask for comments or other suggestions. Listen respectfully.

Suggestions for Conferencing on Another's Portfolio

1. *Listen respectfully.* The other person should do most of the talking.

2. Try to understand the other's goals. If you are not clear about the focus or goals in the portfolio, ask.

3. Try to understand what the person is trying to do to accomplish her/his goals. Ask questions about strategies the person is using.

4. Remember: The focus of any portfolio is growth. Try to understand how the person is growing and improving.

5. Ask other questions to show your interest. For example: What goal is most important to you? Why did you select those goals? What do you think is the best living proof you have in your portfolio? Are you going to change your portfolio in any way? Who else have you conferenced with? Has your portfolio had much meaning for you? What other strategies could help you grow?

SHARING THE LIVING PROOF:
Your Conference Toolbox

Who?	What?	When?	Where?	How?
With yourself	Reflect on your own growth. This type of reflection is often written.	During class time or as a home exercise	In the classroom, or at a quiet spot at home	Teacher allocates a reflection time; you choose a reflection time at home.
With another student	Share your goals, your living proof, and your own reflections with another student. Invite constructive feedback.	During class time	In the classroom	During allocated conferencing time period.
With the teacher	Share your portfolio with the teacher. Discuss your goals and your living proof. Share your reflections. The teacher comments.	Ongoing	In the classroom	You might ask for a conference. The teacher might request a conference.
With a parent; or, with a parent and teacher	Summarize your Living Proof portfolio with your parents and teacher, focusing on your own goals.	Perhaps at a school interview night; perhaps at home	At school; at a quiet place in your home	You are given an opportunity to present your portfolio as a demonstration of improvement, of growth.

Key to Developing Self-Awareness, Worksheet 2

bleak
relaxed
gloomy
forlorn
sensitive
worthless
important
joyful
insignificant
gleeful
dejected
offended
useless
appreciative

p	w	m	h	a	v	r	m	c	t	e	h	b	e	f	u	n	o	o
y	s	q	f	p	x	d	e	j	e	c	t	e	d	v	s	m	o	f
t	e	e	y	p	v	q	m	l	c	o	m	t	u	f	e	n	h	f
b	n	r	o	r	b	m	e	e	a	r	l	o	b	s	l	r	p	e
d	s	q	l	e	g	y	d	p	y	x	m	t	f	s	e	w	p	n
e	i	a	u	c	b	l	f	f	p	d	e	d	e	e	s	n	n	d
f	t	s	f	i	b	l	e	a	k	a	u	d	t	l	s	o	r	e
b	i	a	y	a	v	i	v	e	w	x	y	s	j	h	j	n	o	d
j	v	g	o	t	x	o	h	e	f	z	c	m	g	t	o	o	l	r
l	e	z	j	i	q	r	j	u	n	u	r	a	o	r	i	h	r	t
i	o	z	h	v	x	l	l	h	e	z	l	g	e	o	p	j	o	y
k	b	z	i	e	k	u	k	j	k	r	i	h	b	w	l	k	f	k
j	i	n	s	i	g	n	i	f	i	c	a	n	t	a	g	g	k	j
j	k	r	r	e	t	n	a	t	r	o	p	m	i	m	m	e	q	c

Bibliography

Axline, Virgina M. *Dibs in Search of Self.* New York: Ballantine, 1981.

Branden, Nathaniel. *How to Raise Your Self-Esteem.* New York: Bantam, 1987.

Branden, Nathaniel. *The Psychology of Self-Esteem.* New York: Bantam, 1983.

Coloroso, Barbara. *Kids Are Worth It! Giving Your Child the Gift of Inner Discipline.* Toronto: Somerville House Publishing, 1995.

Cytryn, Leon, and Donald H. McKnew. *Growing Up Sad: Childhood Depression and Its Treatment.* New York: W. W. Norton & Co., 1996.

De Bono, Edward. *Teach Your Child How to Think.* New York: Viking Penguin, 1994.

Dreikurs, Rudolf, et al. *Maintaining Sanity in the Classroom: Classroom Management Techniques.* 2d ed. Bristol, PA: Hemisphere Publishing, 1998.

Ellis, Albert. *Humanistic Psychotherapy: The Rational-Emotive Approach.* New York: McGraw-Hill, 1974.

Fine, Judith. "Research on Teaching Portfolios." Mississauga, ON, 1997.

Gibbs, Nancy. "The EQ Factor." *Time,* 2 October 1995.

Goleman, Daniel. *Emotional Intelligence: Why It Can Matter More Than IQ for Character Health and Lifelong Achievement.* New York: Bantam, 1995.

Heidl-Knap, J. "Reflections." *Portfolio Assessment* (newsletter), November 1995.

Johnson, D. W., and R. T. Johnson. *Reducing School Violence.* Alexandria, VA: Association for Supervision and Curriculum Development, 1995.

Karton, E. "Portfolio Assessment: A Critique." *FWTAO Newsletter,* May/June 1996.

Kerr, Rob. *The Superlative 21st Century Classroom.* Portland, ME: J. Weston Walch, Publisher, 1997.

Kerr, Rob. *Stop and Think: Empowering Students to Manage Behavior.* Portland, ME: J. Weston Walch, Publisher, 1995.

Kerr, Rob. *Positively! Learning to Manage Negative Emotions.* Rev. ed. Portland, ME: J. Weston Walch, Publisher, 1997.

Lerner, Harriet. *The Dance of Anger.* New York: HarperCollins Publishers, 1989.

Metcalf, C. W., and Roma Felible. *Lighten Up: Survival Skills for People Under Pressure.* Reading, MA: Addison-Wesley Publishing Co., 1993.

Peel Board of Education. "A Conversation with Mary Nanavati." *Portfolio Connections* 7 (spring 1997).

Sheppard, B. "Generation X." *Teaching Today* 13 (August/September 1995).

Valencia, S. "A Portfolio Approach to Classroom Reading Assessment: The Whys, Whats, and Hows." *The Reading Teacher* 43 (1990): 338–40.

Recommended Resources

Branden, Nathaniel. *How to Raise Your Self-Esteem*. New York: Bantam, 1987.

Branden, Nathaniel. *The Psychology of Self-Esteem*. New York: Bantam, 1983.

Breheney, Colleen, Vicki Mackrill, and Neville Grady. *Making Peace at Mayfield: A Whole School Approach to Conflict Resolution*. Portsmouth, NH: Heinemann Educational, 1996.

Burnard, Sonia, and Heather Yaxley. *Managing Children's Behaviour in the Classroom: A Practical Guide for Teachers and Students*. Bristol, PA: Taylor & Francis, 1997.

Coloroso, Barbara. *Kids Are Worth It! Giving Your Child the Gift of Inner Discipline*. Toronto: Somerville House Publishing, 1995.

Dreikurs, Rudolf, et al. *Maintaining Sanity in the Classroom: Classroom Management Techniques*. 2d ed. Bristol, PA: Hemisphere Publishing, 1998.

Fine, Esther, et al. *Children as Peacemakers*. Portsmouth, NH: Heinemann Educational, 1995.

Glazer, Susan Mandel, and Carol Smullen Brown. *Portfolios and Beyond: Collaborative Assessment in Reading and Writing*. Norwood, MA: Christopher-Gordon Pubs., Inc., 1993.

Goleman, Daniel. *Emotional Intelligence: Why It Can Matter More Than IQ for Character Health and Lifelong Achievement*. New York: Bantam, 1995.

Gossen, Diane. *Restitution: Restructuring School Discipline*. 2d rev. ed. Chapel Hill, NC: New View Pubns., 1996.

Grant, Janet Millar, Barbara Heffler, and Kadri Mereweather. *Student-Led Conferences: Using Portfolios to Share Learning with Parents*. Markham, ON: Pembroke Publishers, 1995.

Howden, Beverley, and John A. B. Allan. *Caring and Sharing: Facilitating Moral Development in Elementary Schools*. Toronto: Lugus, 1991.

Metcalf, C. W., and Roma Felible. *Lighten Up: Survival Skills for People Under Pressure*. Reading, MA: Addison-Wesley Publishing Co., 1993.

Metropolitan Toronto School Board. *Challenging Ourselves: Gender Equity and Violence-Free Relationships*. Markham, ON: Pembroke Publishers, 1996.

Porter, Carol, and Janell Cleland. *The Portfolio as a Learning Strategy*. Portsmouth, NH: Boynton/Cook Pubs., 1994.

Rigby, Ken. *Bullying in Schools and What to Do About It*. Markham, ON: Pembroke Publishers, 1998.

Russell, Anita M. *Self-Esteem*. Winnipeg, MB: Peguis, 1989.

Stones, Rosemary. *Don't Pick on Me: How to Handle Bullying*. Markham, ON: Pembroke Publishers, 1993.

Vincent, Philip Fitch. *Developing Character in Students: A Primer*. Chapel Hill, NC: New View Pubns., 1994.

Willis, M. V. *Reclaiming America's Children: Raising and Educating Morally Healthy Kids*. Vero Beach, FL: Ocean East Publishing, 1991.

Index